THE SCHOLAR BUDGET

GUIDE TO PAYING FOR COLLEGE

THE SCHOLAR BUDGET

GUIDE TO PAYING FOR COLLEGE

by

Rockell Bartoli

Dedication

To the students that are ready to earn a debt-free college degree and live a financially savvy life. Don't grow weary in doing the hard work now. Your future self will be grateful.

Contents

Dedication   v

1. Before She Knew It   1

2. The FAFSA   5

3. Scholarships   13

4. Dual Enrollment   23

5. Employer Tuition Assistance   31

6. How About Them Grades, Though?   39

7. Sports, Academics, Arts, and Extra-Curricular Activities   45

8. Test Me   49

9. Learn, Earn, and Pay with Tuition Remission   57

10. The Side Hustle   63

11. Programs That Pay   67

12. Crowdfunding For Education   83

13. Be All That You Can Be with A Debt Free Degree   87

14. You Can Save Something   93

15. If You Have No Other Choice   95

16. If You Don't Take Action, This Could Be Your Story   103

17. What Is Your Game Plan?   125

1.

Before She Knew It

This was the goal, this was the dream, this was what the hard work and tears were for. Before she knew it, she was adulting with a degree in elementary education and a master's in school counseling. She was a high school guidance counselor, happily married with two kids, living in a quiet neighborhood less than ten minutes from her mema's house (that's her grandma). Everything she put on her vision board and prayed about seemed to be coming to life. She was living her dream, all while drowning in a nightmare of what started as $60,000 in student loan debt. Then, before she knew it, it grew to $80,000 in under ten years, and with all the loops the Public Service Loan Forgiveness Program seemed to be making her jump through, it felt like there was no end in sight.

How did she get to this point, you ask? Well, she relied on student loans to cover a large portion of her education without doing the research. She decided to attend a private university vs. public, she borrowed more money than she needed, she didn't do much to avoid student loans, and she really didn't think about the impact the student loans would have on her life and future as she signed the dotted line to seal the deal on a decade long journey of paying off her student loan debt. She had a dream and a goal of graduating from college, but no effective plan to pay for it. She didn't have parents that put aside money in a college savings plan or a lavish scholarship to offer her a full ride. She wonders why she didn't take the time to repeatedly ask herself this one very important question:

Am I doing everything possible to pay for college and avoid student loan debt?

Who is she?
She is me.
Rockell Bartoli.

My advice to you is to do **EVERYTHING** possible to steer clear of going down the same path I did. Be different. Plan, prepare, and work now so you can graduate from college with little to no student loan debt later.

By the time you're done reading this book (and I do hope you read it from start to finish), you will be equipped with numerous strategies to do everything possible to pay for college while minimizing your need for student loans. You will now be able to put together your own unique game plan to pay for college, and the best part is that you don't have to rely on one single strategy. Also, because I know that we are humans, and sometimes, we need to hear the same advice and life-altering lessons from different people before it really makes sense, I've included snippets of interviews I've conducted with amazing people, to help you understand how these college paying strategies work. Read this book all the way through. It will be a game changer for you.

Take action, my friend, so your journey to paying for college doesn't replicate those of Chapter 16. Let's Do This!

2.

The FAFSA

I saw the bold letters on the posters that were hanging in the counselor's office. It was actually posted in other areas around the school as well. The closer I got to senior year, the more the letters appeared, and the more the letters rolled off my counselor and cap advisor's tongue. The FAFSA seemed like it was going to be a very important part of my college journey, and would turn my dreams into a reality. By the way, did I tell you what my dreams were? Well, my plan and big dreams were to go to college to become an elementary school teacher, meet a guy with really good DNA (because I'm already cute, so if he's cute, then our kids are guaranteed to be cute … LOL), get married, have four kids, buy a really big house, travel, and live happily ever after. Fast forward to today, and well, I've accomplished my mission of becoming an elementary teacher. You better believe my hubby has that good DNA; two kids sometimes feels like four. Big houses are overrated when you realize you have to clean the whole thing. Yes, we travel, and I have joy. Life is not perfect, but I'm happy, content, and grateful. So, back to the FAFSA. Like many of my peers, I definitely procrastinated in filling out my FAFSA application. I think at some point in time, I realized that if I don't complete this paper, then I'm not going to college. Yes! You heard me right, complete the paper application. Back in my days, which was actually 2003, the majority of us completed the FAFSA by hand, with a pencil and paper application. Whether it be a paper application or computer application, completing the FAFSA was no easy task. It was really confusing and overwhelming. Believe me when I say I made a ton of errors, and being a first-generation college student with no adequate support at home made this whole process even more difficult. Eventually, I finally completed it accurately and was able to secure the aid I needed for most of my undergraduate degree.

Oftentimes, we'll find challenges and barriers embedded in the things we MUST do in order to move forward, and the FAFSA is no different. We know we MUST complete the application in order to secure funding for college, but mindset barriers and personal circumstances can leave us feeling defeated and putting the FAFSA on the back burner. On one hand, you can have a student that feels like they won't receive any aid other than loans because of their parents' income. On the other hand, you can have a student that can't complete their application because the parent has not provided their tax information or followed any of the other steps to help complete the process. Let's not forget the student that just feels overwhelmed by the process and doesn't have enough support and accountability to get everything done. Nevertheless, I believe that when there is a will, there is a way, and that often includes being able to self-advocate and tap into ALL of our resources to get the help we need. No matter what grade level you are in, you can start getting prepared for the FAFSA and get the assistance you need if you find yourself unable to complete your application.

Here are some FAFSA Completion Tips:

- Don't wait until junior and senior year to visit www. studentaid.gov. The earlier you and your parents start reading and getting familiar with the FAFSA and how it works, the easier the process will be when it's actually time for you to apply.

- There are various blogs, YouTube channels, and content you can Google to help you learn about the FAFSA application process.

- The FAFSA is the gateway to all other funding, so even if you think you won't receive any aid other than student loans, it's in your best interest to complete it and gain access to other scholarships and funding opportunities.

- If you're done with trying to figure it out on your own, you can reach out to your school counselor, college prep counselor, teacher, or coach to provide you with more support or resources.

- When in doubt, you can always contact the Federal Student Aid Information Center at 1-800-433-3243, or visit their website at www.studentaid.gov to send an email.

The Scholarship Momma sat down with me and gave me some pretty solid tips about the FAFSA. By the way, feel free to connect with Ms. Theresa Harris on social @ iamscholarshipmomma or www.scholarshipmomma.com.

Me: What is the worst-case scenario if a student does not complete their FAFSA? What happens to that student who wants to go to college, but for whatever reason, doesn't submit their application?

Scholarship Momma: The worst-case scenario, if you don't complete the FAFSA is, you're not eligible for any federal student aid. Once you become ineligible for federal student aid, then the question becomes, how will you pay for college? A lot of colleges also offer institutional grants, which we call college grants or grants that you don't have to pay back. For those grants, a lot of colleges look at the FAFSA as well. If they don't have any record of the FAFSA on file, then you will become ineligible for the aid that they are offering you. That's why it's really important that students and families complete the FAFSA, so you can be eligible for federal aid as well as any aid that the colleges are giving. Some scholarship providers also want students to complete the FASFA as well. It's a possibility that you might be ineligible for scholarships, too.

Rockell: That is all so true! What would you say students should do if they hit roadblocks and obstacles while completing their FAFSA? For example, those who are no longer in touch with their parents but need their parents' tax information, or foster kids. Or just filling out the application in general, like, not knowing what to do or what some of the questions mean. Or doing the application and getting it rejected because they constantly get things done incorrectly, and then they get frustrated. What would you say are some resources or some things students should do when they start hitting roadblocks?

Scholarship Momma: The FAFSA makes allowances for dependent students whose parents are unwilling to share financial information. What happens is that the FAFSA will reject the application. Some schools will ask for more information, but ultimately, it's the student's responsibility to inform the school that the parent won't provide information. What I would suggest for the students is that they really talk to the school, the financial aid administrators at the school that they are interested in going to, and explain the situation to them. If it's a case where the parent doesn't want to cooperate, but the student does know the parent, then what happens is, the student becomes eligible for financial aid, but not that much. They actually lose out.

As it pertains to being a foster child or ward of the court, if at any time after the age of thirteen, the student was in foster care/ ward of the court, a student is considered independent, therefore, no parental information will be required. The FAFSA also has information boxes to help guide students through successfully completing the FAFSA. The federal student aid information center is another resource to assist students with questions. Students can call 1-800-4FED-AID (1-800-433-3243).

Lastly, a new resource the U.S. Department of Education

just added is Aidan, which is FSA Virtual Assistant (Chatbot). Aidan is available to answer questions about the FAFSA and federal student aid twenty-four hours a day.

Rockell: I see. What if a student gets absolutely nothing after completing their FAFSA, and they're feeling down like, "Oh my God, how am I going to pay for college?" What would you say to those students who are only getting loans from the FAFSA?

Scholarship Momma: My next step for those students would be to offer a few options. I tell them to apply for scholarships. That's the number one thing I tell them to do—to apply for scholarships if they don't want to fund their entire education with student loans. Not only that, you have to apply for scholarships the entire time you are in school. At that point, I start trying to share strategies with them. Are you currently employed? If so, does your employer offer tuition reimbursement? If your parents are employed, and you are a dependent student, I tell students to ask their parents if their job offers scholarships. Many employers do, but some employees (parents) aren't aware. So I ask them, "Have you saved any money? Is there a possibility that you can help pay towards college without having to take out student loans as well?" Another question that I asked them as well is are they going to work? "Are you going to work during school?" Whether it be a federal work-study or a part-time job, to lessen that amount of student loan debt. Then I always tell them to ask the school if they have more money. A lot of times, families feel that because they're not eligible for any aid, the

PELL grant, etc., that they're not eligible for anything else. That includes scholarships as well, but that's not true. There are just scholarships for need-based students as well as merit scholarships. I tell them, "Ask the school if they have any more money," and actually, a tip or a pro tip I would say too, is to keep asking. When you ask them in the fall, maybe go back and ask in November, because an inside tip is, some of those students do not come to school as they're projected to, and that money goes back.

3.

Scholarships

Why do you want to go to college? How has your education contributed to who you are today? Choose a person you admire and explain why. From a financial standpoint, what impact would this scholarship have on your education? These are just a few of the questions you might need to answer when completing your next scholarship application.

Scholarships are golden for so many reasons:

1. You don't need to pay them back. Yep, you get to use that money for your education or educational expenses, and not pay it back.

2. It's payback for earning good grades, being involved in your community, being a great athlete, having a talent, overcoming obstacles, thinking outside of the box, being a good human being, or just shooting your shot, even when you thought you wouldn't get it.

3. They can significantly decrease your need for student loans.

4. Did I already say that you DON'T have to pay it back?

So, I want to encourage you to A.B.A.F.S 'Always Be Applying for Scholarships,' and don't wait until your senior year of high school either. Believe it or not, there are scholarships for middle and high school students, so why wait? Really, why are you waiting? Oh! I know. I've heard from some students that they don't consider themselves to be good or strong writers; they don't believe that they'll actually win, or better yet, they just haven't made the time to complete a scholarship application. If you don't consider yourself to be a good writer or you don't believe that you'll be chosen, then I understand how self-doubt can immediately stop you dead in your tracks. Well, let me help you reverse some of those thoughts so you can get those applications completed. Here me out ... you don't **NEED** to be a great writer to develop a scholarship-winning essay. You can work at getting better through each essay and attempt. Just like becoming physically fit requires consistency, developing a scholarship-winning essay requires the same thing–consistency. Here are a few tips to ensure that you get better at developing these essays and increase your chances of securing multiple scholarships.

1. **ALWAYS** type or write your response on a Word document or paper before entering your response on the application itself. The key here is to have your essay proofread and edited by your teacher, counselor, parent, or someone who can give you sound advice on how to make your essay better. I have also paid a small fee on sites like fiverr.com and upwork.com to have my work proofread and edited. I'm not the greatest writer out there, so I need feedback and help, catching my own errors and making corrections.

2. As you're writing your essay, **ALWAYS** take a break to go back to the question and read what you've written so far

to make sure you're on the right track to answering the question. When you're sharing your own story, it's easy to go off on a tangent and lose sight of what you should be writing about.

3. Your first 2-3 sentences are what I like to call a **"LEAD MAGNET."** Why? Well, this helps the person reading your essay to be intrigued and naturally want to read more of your response. The goal here is to not sound like everyone else but to express the beginning of your thoughts by being a descriptive storyteller. You can also use analogies and quotes to help get your point and answer across to the reader. Get the reader's attention!

4. If the scholarship is giving you up to 500 words to express your answer, use as many of those words as you can without adding fluff. Trust me, the reader can sense fluff. Instead, use descriptive words, give examples, share your story, and answer the question. Try not to be the applicant who submitted a 200-word response to a 500-word essay, even if it says you don't have to use all 500 words.

5. Get busy - literally - and get involved in things that you are interested in. Join and be an active member of clubs at school and in other organizations. Use your gift and talents as an athlete, artist, musician, writer, speaker, or gamer. Whatever it is, showcase what you're doing in school and outside of school. You can use your experiences in your college application essays and your scholarship application essays.

Now, if you're struggling with finding the time to apply for scholarships, then I want to remind you that we **MAKE** time for the things we want. When I'm faced with something I don't want to do, I can oftentimes find an excuse as to why I can't do it right now, but let one of my friends or hubby say, "Let's go out to eat, shop, or watch a good Netflix show," then I can find every excuse to make room in my schedule even when I have other things that might be a priority. I know applying for scholarships isn't the most enjoyable thing in the world, but I also know you can find time to apply. You might need to make a sacrifice by spending less time on social media, playing video games, watching TV, hanging out with friends or your significant other, and dedicating (insert a doable number) amount of hours applying for scholarships. We can also revisit the reason why it's important to A.B.A.F.S. (Always Be Applying for Scholarships) because we want to minimize our need to take out and rely on student loans. It's literally a crisis right now on these student loan streets, with hundreds of thousands of people knee-deep in student loan debt. Shoot your shot, friend, multiple times every year you're a student. If you think of it this way, you have eight years to apply for scholarships if you start as early as 9th grade. You can do this!

Oh, and did I forget to mention that the more scholarships you apply for and write essays for, the easier the process becomes? Eventually, you'll identify scholarships with similar essay questions, and you can take some of what you've already written for a previous scholarship and add it to your new scholarship essay.

Check out what my multiple scholarship-winning friend, Logan, had to say about his scholarship journey.

Rockell: Hello, Logan, what school do you attend and what are you majoring in?

Logan: I go to The Honors College at FIU, Florida International University, and I'm majoring in political science. I'm getting a minor in international relations and certificates in communications and ethics law in society.

Rockell: That is pretty awesome. I know that's quite a bit of work.

Logan: Yeah. And I'm hoping to graduate in three years.

Rockell: Oh, look at that. I love those goals. So, when it comes to scholarships, how many scholarships did you apply for when you were in high school?

Logan: So, when I was in high school, I probably applied to about 50 to 60 scholarships.

Rockell: Wow. That is a lot. And how many of them did you win? How much did you win?

Logan: I probably won about six or seven, which was like 20-25,000 dollars.

Rockell: Awesome. And so, let me ask, did your mindset play a role in you applying for scholarships? Or, was this just like easy peasy for you?

Logan: No. So, this whole process was really challenging for me because when I was applying, COVID came, and s o, that really threw off my plans because I was hoping to go to school to play sports. I remember, the day before school was canceled, I had a meeting with our coach on that Monday at FIU for track. And then, after that, I lost contact with him. It was really hard. So, I'm really thankful that I applied for the scholarships because without them, I would've been out of luck - completely out of luck - because I had nothing else planned, really.

Rockell: Right. And were there times when you felt like, "I don't want to write another essay, or I don't want to apply for another scholarship?" Did that ever happen?

Logan: Absolutely. I mean, scholarships are not always easy. Some of them are really long and intense, like multiple, multiple essays to do. So, it's not fun sometimes. But, you really have to keep pushing through it because, at the end of the day, you're trying to benefit yourself.

Rockell: Right. And let me ask, why do you think you won the scholarships that you won?

Logan: I would say that I've tried my best to create a story to say why I'm unique, why my story's different. And that's what I would advocate for everybody that is applying for scholarships- to share why you are unique. What do you do that stands out from everybody else? What separates you? And just, really focusing on my story. That's really what the basis of my scholarships was.

Rockell: Awesome. So, having a unique story, finding your story, and then using that. And as you were writing these essays, did it become a little bit easier over time, because of your story? Or, did you have to start from scratch every time?

Logan: No, it was easier because you really just focus on those main talking points, of what you really see in yourself. And then, what you believe in and what you want for the world. Because a lot of them are like, "Oh, what do you want to do? What changes do you want to make? What changes do you want to see in society?" So, I shared how I worked at the Special Olympics, and how I'm always fighting for inclusion - So, that was really my story. And then, there were the challenges I went through and stuff. So, I would say that once you get the basis, everything else becomes easier along the way.

Rockell: Awesome. And so, what would you say to any high school student right now, whether they're a ninth grader or a senior, so that they can position themselves to qualify for scholarships? What advice would you give to those students right now?

Logan: My main advice would be not to put all your eggs in one basket. Because I did that, I really depended on sports for a while. And then, as I got along in high school, I was like, "Oh, maybe I should start doing other things." So then, I tried to become well-rounded. It's very important to become well-rounded and not to be discouraged by not winning a scholarship. Just keep trying, keep trying. There are so many scholarships out there, and there's so many opportunities to not just get discouraged by one scholarship.

Rockell: Right. Can you elaborate a little bit more on well-rounded? What does that mean for a ninth grader coming into high school? You tell them to be well-rounded. Can you just go into a little more detail as to what that means?

Logan: Absolutely. So, I would say focus on academics, athletics, and community service. If athletics isn't in your background, there's still so many other things you could do. Like the Special Olympics, you don't have to just be an athlete to be a part of it. There's so many different community service activities, and then, your academics are really important, no matter what.

Rockell: Perfect. Also, do you think a person has to be a straight "A" student in order to receive scholarships? Do I have to be super perfect? What are your thoughts on that?

Logan: I do not think that at all. I think it's more about the story and how you portray yourself and how you really think about making an impact. Because, my sister is in the hospital homebound program, and she didn't get the best test scores; but since she's such a well-rounded person, we're really hopeful that she'll be able to win some scholarships through that. So, I would say that it's not all about the grades. It's not all about the pretty grades and the perfect transcript. Sometimes, it's also about what you do in the community and the impact you're making.

Rockell: That's what's up! So, as a junior, just minutes away from graduating from college, are you still applying for scholarships? Or, are you done with that journey?

Logan: Yes, I am still applying. Actually, during this winter break, I've applied for two more scholarships. And then, I would apply for scholarships at the school just to hopefully win because funding's really important, and I'm trying my best to save money. So, applying for scholarships is important. No matter if you already won a lot of them, you have to reapply, too. So, just because you win a couple in your freshman year doesn't mean to stop applying.

What limiting thoughts are stopping you from applying for scholarships, and why is it important for you to reframe your thoughts so you can move forward?

_____

_____

_____

_____

_____

What sacrifices can you make in your schedule to complete and submit at least 3-4 scholarships per month?

_____

_____

_____

_____

_____

_____

4.

Dual Enrollment

Nothing is worse than missing out on a really good deal. It's kind of like your favorite store or company offering a BOGO and you miss the email or totally forget about the offer. Not sure what I mean? Well, let's use one of my favorite fast-food spots, Chick-Fil-A. Imagine Chick-fil-A or your favorite restaurant sending you an email to get a buy one, get one free meal, and then you totally forget about it. Let's pause right here and let that pain sink in. Ok, maybe it's not that serious, but you get my point. That's how I feel about Dual-Enrollment. Boy, did I miss out on a super fantastic opportunity to earn college credits and fasttrack my way to graduating college. I really dropped the ball on this one, friend, but there's no point in crying over spilled milk. Dual-Enrollment is an amazingly smart way to decrease your need for student loans because this program saves you time and money. The name of this program also differs from state to state, but you're basically looking for an early college program for high school students.

Dual-enrollment is packed with tons of other amazing benefits, like:

1. Preparing for college! College classes give you the hands-on experience to know what you can expect even before you step foot on campus.

2. Exploration! Oftentimes, students go to college not

really knowing what kind of degree they want to pursue. By taking classes while in high school, you explore your options through the classes you get to take and you get to connect with college advisors.

3. You're technically already a college student, so you can access the college resources and even some clubs and campus events.

Now, the Dual-Enrollment process and guidelines vary from state to state, so, do yourself a favor and check with your school counselor or advisor to get more information and learn if you qualify. If you find that you don't qualify right now, don't let that stop you. Sit with your counselor and create a game plan to increase your GPA or pass any necessary test required for you to participate. Dual-Enrollment, my friends, is a really great way to pay for college!

After speaking to Kailyn Moss, who took advantage of Dual-Enrollment, I was reminded of why this option is a game-changer in helping pay for college.

Rockell: Kailyn, what is Dual-Enrollment in your opinion?

Kailyn: So, for me, Dual-Enrollment, I don't like to think of it as college classes even though it is, because it can sound scary. You feel like it's harder. So, I really just like to think of it as a few more classes that I'm taking outside of my normal high school schedule that will end up saving me lots and lots of money and time in the long run.

Rockell: I understand that. College classes while you're in high school can initially feel a little intimidating. How did you learn about Dual-Enrollment?

Kailyn: I learned about it from my high school counselors mostly in my 10th grade year, because that's when you really start to take AP classes. AP classes aren't for everybody, so they were telling us that as an alternative to still get college credit is to do Dual-Enrollment instead.

Rockell: I see. How many classes have you taken so far?

Kailyn: I've been doing Dual-Enrollment for two years and seven semesters. So, it's been around twenty-three or twenty-four classes.

Rockell: Twenty-four classes or credits????

Kailyn: Twenty-three classes. I have over sixty credits. Yeah.

Rockell: Whaaaaaat? Girl, you are awesome!!!

Kailyn: This is my last semester before I get my AA degree.

Rockell: Oh my God, that's awesome. Why did you decide to take Dual-Enrollment classes?

Kailyn: I've known since elementary school that I wanted a career in the medical field. When I began to look at all of the schooling, I realized it would take like seven to ten years, and how much money you had to put into it. I was trying to find a way to not only shorten the length, but also, the amount of money that I had to spend. I wanted these classes and started getting some of them out of the way - at least, the beginning courses, so that I can get ahead and save money.

Rockell: Love it. How do you balance your time with regular school and Dual-Enrollment?

Kailyn: I definitely still kind of struggle with it a little bit, because it does become a lot sometimes. What I decided to do is write down and plan everything. At the beginning, at least for college, you get your syllabus with a list of things that you're going to do in the class. The syllabus also gives you an idea of the time and dates that things are going to be due. I try to plan out everything. I know I'm going to be in the classroom this time. I even try to put time for studying, or the time I plan on going to sleep, and what free time I need. I make sure when I do plan it, I give myself time ahead, before assignments are due to try and get everything done on time. It's been working, but sometimes, it's kind of hard, and I stray away a bit.

Rockell: It's never perfect, but you're doing it. Do you use a digital planner or a paper planner?

Kailyn: I personally like to have the planner right in front of me and write in it. So, I have a planner that I got from Target; a physical one. But there's definitely templates you can download and digital planners.

Rockell: Perfect. What would you say are the benefits of taking college-level classes while you're in high school?

Kailyn: Other than the fact that you get to save money and time later on, you also get to meet people who are older than you and more experienced in the college department. You get to talk to them, get advice from them before you have to be full-time in college and you're just scrambling. You get to see them and where you want to be later, and take advice from them. You also get to feel out the college setting. If you don't like it, you still have time to slow down and try a different route. Also, if you don't know what major you want to be in yet, you can try to start taking some classes to see how you feel about certain majors.

Rockell: Awesome. So, based on what you're saying, you save money. You save time. You get to network with people that are years ahead of you, and they can give you guidance and advice. And it's a really good way to test the waters to see if college or a specific major is for me. Does that sound right?

Kailyn: Yes.

Rockell: What advice would you give to students that want to participate in Dual-Enrollment? What would you say to that ninth grader, tenth grader, or even that middle schooler, who's reading this book right now? What would you say to them so they can position themselves to qualify and take courses like you are?

Kailyn: Definitely ask questions and do your research. Don't just wait for it to be told to you. If you want to do it, you go and look for it. See what you need to qualify, and what you need to study. To start Dual-Enrollment, you have to take the PERT exam (for Miami Dade County Public School students). Try to see what's on the PERT exam, and try to start studying early. Also, if it is something you want to do, you have to make sure that you want to do it and you're ready to do it, because once you start these classes, this is going on your college GPA. If you do badly at the beginning, it's going to tarnish the GPA, and it's going to be really hard to bring it up. If they understand that part and they're ready to do it and ready to commit, then I feel like they should do it because it's free, and will help them in the long run. You can have a whole degree when you're graduating high school.

Rockell: Right, and that's what you're going to graduate with. You're going to graduate with your AA. Is that correct?

Kailyn: I'm actually going to have my AA before I even get my high school diploma, but I have to wait because you can't have an AA without a high school diploma. Technically, I would be done with my AA before I even finish high school.

Rockell: Oh, my goodness, you're a high school senior getting ready to graduate with an AA. Congratulations to you!

Kailyn: Thank you.

Who do you need to contact at your school to participate in Dual-Enrollment?

_____

_____

_____

_____

If you don't qualify for Dual-Enrollment right now, what can you do to reverse that (improve grades, scores, study, etc.)?

_____

_____

_____

_____

5.

Employer Tuition Assistance

I honestly can't recall how I stumbled across it, because social media wasn't really a thing then, except for Myspace. But now that I think about it, it was actually posted in the newspaper. I read that AT&T was hiring a telephone sales representative for the Yellow Pages. I had worked at PRC (Precision Response Corporation) for several months as a customer service representative for Direct TV—throwback satellite dishes. That's also where I met my husband. Oh, the good old days. Anyhow, at this point, I felt comfortable talking to people on the phone, so I figured I should shoot my shot and apply for this position. Before I could even get the interview, I had to complete my application, submit my bare resume, and wait patiently for a response. Then I had to take a test that would show if I had the skills to get the job done. I can't remember any of the questions, but I do remember feeling nervous and excited at the same time.

A few weeks later, I got the phone call! I was sitting in my English 101 class at Miami Dade College, and I quietly stepped out of the room to accept the call. A lady from the HR department called me to verify some things on my application, and informed me that I would receive another phone call within a couple of days to let me know about my status. A couple of days went by, and that call did come through. We set up the date for the interview, and I practiced and prepared a little in front of the mirror, fumbling over my words and eager to get the interview over with. I also had one of my friends ask me a series of basic interview questions to get ready for the big day. That morning, I put on a business skirt and a blouse, and made myself look as professional as possible. When I got to the building, the security guard asked me for my ID, checked me in, and I patiently waited for someone to come downstairs to escort me upstairs. As we got on the elevator and the doors closed, I could feel my heart beating inside of my chest. Do you get nervous before an interview? Shoot, I sure do. We exited the elevator and made our way to the hallway that would lead to the room for the interview. On the way there, I could already see that this was the place I wanted to be. I just felt it! So, I entered the room, and there were three people waiting for me. I sat in front of them and reminded myself to take deep breaths. I felt like I had something lodged in my throat, and I kept swallowing my spit to get rid of that feeling. Some of you know that feeling I'm talking about, right? They asked me the interview questions, and I answered all of them to the best of my ability. I think we were in the interview for about 15-20 mins. After it was done, I stood up and shook each person's hand before thanking them and exiting the room.

A couple of days of prayers, and checking my phone every two minutes later, and I got the job! This was going to be one of the best jobs of my life ... I could feel it. I can honestly say today that it actually was. The money I made was absolutely amazing for a nineteen-year-old, and the friends I made were some of the best that you can find. However, that tuition reimbursement was something I didn't even expect, but it was exactly what I needed as a first-generation college student paying for college on my own. When I found that this was one of the many benefits of being an employee with this company, I filled out all the forms and counted it as a blessing that not only was I getting paid really good money, I was also getting help to pay for college. Talk about a win-win situation.

This is an opportunity that many students like you can take advantage of, too! Employer tuition assistance programs are out there, but you must do your research. This is another great way to pay for college, and you don't have to pay the money back like you would with a student loan, unless your employer has a special requirement in which you have to commit to working with them for a certain number of years to accept the tuition assistance, which isn't something the majority of employers do. The bottom line is that this is a benefit specific employers offer, and it's worth looking into.

I was so excited to hear how Walmart is helping their employees earn a debt-free degree. Lakesia gave me the inside scoop on why Walmart's employee tuition program is worth looking into.

Rockell: What's the name of the company or organization that you're the Human Resource person for?

Lakesia: I work for a company that is owned by Walmart. It's called Bonobos. Under that company, Walmart has a program where they pay a hundred percent of college tuition and books for their associates. Over the next five years, Walmart is going to invest over $1 billion in career-driven training and development.

Rockell: Wow! That is pretty awesome.

Lakesia: Yes. This means approximately 1.5 million of our part-time and full-time Walmart and Sam's Club associates in the U.S. will be able to earn college degrees or learn trade skills without the burden of college debt.

Rockell: Are you going to take advantage of this opportunity, or is it something that you don't need right now?

Lakesia: I am not in need of that opportunity at this time. I want those who are just deciding what they want to do with their lives and careers to take advantage of this program.

Rockell: Awesome. What is the criteria, more or less?

Lakesia: It's a little too detailed for me to go into full depth, but you, of course, have to be working at a Walmart store.

Rockell: Of course! There is a probationary period, right? You have to be working with the company for a certain amount of time before the benefit starts?

Lakesia: Yeah. You do have to go through a probationary period, like with any job.

Lakesia: Walmart partners with different universities, and they're always expanding, looking for new opportunities to support their associates with the different colleges that are OK with paying for certain things, so students don't have to come out of pocket with those expenses. I think it's an excellent, excellent program.

Rockell: Absolutely! So, there are specific colleges that Walmart has a partnership with. Can an employee also choose whatever college they're going to go to?

Lakesia: Right now, there are specific colleges that Walmart does have partnerships with, but I always like to say, if you don't ask, you don't know. If there's a college that you're interested in and you want to see if that can be approved, ask. I would always ask. If you never ask, the answer is no. If you do, there's a 50% chance. You can say something like, "Hey, have we ever considered adding this to our list of colleges?" I'm sure somebody else is thinking the same thing you're thinking.

Lakesia: Then also, something that Walmart is doing for employees that are high school students is giving them free access to ACT and SAT prep.

Rockell: What! When did that start?

Lakesia: Don't quote me on the exact date, but it's a part of their Live Better You program.

Rockell: Oh! That's awesome. Awesome. Awesome. Would you say that this is a good strategy to consider as an undergrad student, or even a high school student getting ready to go to college, and they know that they're going to be working while attending school? Do you think that this is a good strategy to add to their toolbox when they're thinking about, "Okay, how am I going to pay for college and reduce my student loan need?"

Lakesia: Oh, absolutely. Because it's basically, you're working and then, because you're working, you also are paying for school. It's not like you're working and getting all these student loans at the same time, so when you get out of school, you have this big debt.

Rockell: Would you give any suggestions, or tips, to anyone who wants to start working for Walmart? How can they position themselves to qualify? Is it just a matter of filling out the application and submitting the resume? What would you say to a high school student getting ready to graduate, and who's about to start next semester, and thinking about getting a job with Walmart? What would you say to that person to be in the best position to get the job?

Lakesia: I would definitely follow up. Once you've put in your resume, follow up. See who the hiring manager is. Find them on LinkedIn. See how you can send them a message and let them know how excited you are about the potential opportunity. People think cover letters are dead, do a cover letter. Express your interests. Why do you want to work for them? Those small little things make a big difference.

Do a quick Google search to see if you have any businesses close to you or the college you will be attending that offer tuition assistance or tuition reimbursement and list them below. A few of my favorite employers with this awesome incentive are Target, AT&T and Home Depot.

_____

_____

_____

_____

_____

Now go apply!

6.

How About Them Grades, Though?

Listennnnnnnn! Rockell Bartoli didn't have the best grades in the world. If you look at the picture below, you'll catch a glimpse of what my high school career and grades looked like. I would consider myself an average student that had the potential to do better, but the truth is, I was distracted and I was not consistent about putting forth maximum effort into my academics. What was I distracted by, you ask? Wellllll, a boyfriend, a part-time job, and friends. I was too distracted by the things that were going on around me that I failed to consistently study, attend class, take notes, practice, etc.

I lived with my mom and siblings when I was in high school, and my mom didn't really stress me about my grades. No one was asking me for a report card or a progress report. I think the fact that I stayed off the radar as far as not getting into trouble and my teachers weren't calling home, made my mom and grandma feel like I was "good" and I could handle it. However, that was the total opposite. I needed someone to check me and hold me accountable. I needed someone to be all up in my gradebook and remind me that I needed to focus on my education and not a boy, money, or friends. Your grades matter, and what matters the most is the amount of effort and energy you put into earning your grades. Not everyone is going to be a straight "A" student, but everyone can try and do basic but important things like studying, reading, taking notes, asking questions, and participating in class.

Your grades don't just show you and the colleges what you're capable of; your grades can open the door to money that you can use to pay for your college education. Say hello to my little friend called "merit scholarships." I know you've probably heard of merit scholarships before, but I want to provide you with a little more insight into what a merit scholarship is and how you can secure one.

What are merit scholarships: According to findaid. org, "Merit scholarships are typically awarded on the basis of academic, athletic, or artistic merit, in addition to special interests. Some merit scholarships also consider financial needs, but rewarding talent is the primary objective."

Let me break it down even more: Let's say you've been putting in the work to excel academically (studying, taking challenging courses, asking for help when you need it, staying up late to prepare for the test, attending tutoring sessions, and focusing on producing the best grades possible). Is this you? Then a merit scholarship might be right for you.

We'll talk about leveling up your game to qualify for athletic, artistic, and special interest merit scholarships in the next chapter.

How can you increase your chances of receiving an academic merit scholarship? Put forth maximum effort and do your absolute best to earn and maintain good grades and great test scores! You don't need to be perfect to earn an academic merit scholarship, but your grades need to show that you excel academically along with all the other awesome things you're doing as a student.

This can be done by:

- Forming and using good study habits.
- Taking notes.
- Reading.
- Studying and preparing for test.
- Get tutoring or extra help when you realize that you can't do it on your own.
- Surrounding yourself with other like-minded people that you can study with and motivate each other.
- Joining and being an active member of various school clubs and community organizations.
- Community service.
- Leadership.

There are also merit scholarships that are given based on financial need, but they will also be looking at your academics and GPA. I mean, wouldn't you want to make sure a student is serious about their education and has the potential to do well before handing over 10, 15, or 20,000 dollars? Your hard work and dedication can pay for your college education!

How can you apply for a merit scholarship? There are some profit and non-profit organizations that offer really generous merit scholarships. These organizations are often looking for high-achieving students that also demonstrate a financial need. You can do a Google search for merit-based scholarships or communicate with your counselor about these kinds of scholarships.

You will also find that many schools offer merit-based scholarships. You typically apply to the school you're interested in, and if they offer merit-based scholarships, you can be considered for it after they review your application and transcript. Keep in mind that they will be looking at your GPA, test scores, and class rank. The sooner you apply, the sooner you can be considered.

Plus, if you do obtain an academic merit scholarship, know that there are often certain stipulations or guidelines that you must follow to maintain your scholarship, like maintaining your college GPA.

Please know that you are capable of excelling academically, but if you allow the distractions to get the best of you, you'll miss out on an opportunity to utilize an academic merit scholarship to help pay for college.

List five things you can start doing now to improve your chances of securing an academic merit scholarship, and do some research to see if the colleges you're interested in offer merit scholarships!!!

_____

_____

_____

_____

_____

7.

Sports, Academics, Arts, and Extra-Curricular Activities

There was something about the game of kick-ball that always got me excited. As we spread out on the field in elementary school, physical education always started with stretching. Then, on kick-ball days, there would be two team captains assigned by the P.E teacher. The two captains would stand in front of the rest of the class and were given the task of choosing other students to join their team. Whenever I was called to be a captain, I would choose my close friends and then the students who could run fast. Whenever it was my turn to be chosen, in my head I would be like, "Pick me, pick me, you know I'm one of the fastest." I never said it out loud, though. Eventually, I put two and two together and realized that I really was a decent runner. I joined the track team in middle school, and I was this close to joining the long-distance team at my high school, but the way that the Miami sun was set up on those first couple of days, my high school self was not having it. My friend Jeanelle and I were both like, "It is way too hot out here to be running," and immediately quit. I would like to think if I continued running track and sharpening my skills, maybe it could have led to a merit scholarship or even a regular scholarship, but I gave it up before I could turn the possibility into a reality.

Did I also mention that, along with being a pretty decent runner, I was in the magnet program at my middle school for chorus and I had a thing for drawing? Well, now you know and the reason I'm sharing this with you is because I know you have a talent or two that you've tapped into or you're not fully embracing. These talents and gifts that you have can also help you pay for college. There are merit scholarships that are given to students just like you. I want to encourage you to grow as a student, but also grow in your athletic ability, artistic ability, leadership ability, and anything else you might be uber passionate about. Merit scholarships are offered to high-achieving academic students, and they are also offered to students excelling in sports, arts, and other various extracurricular activities.

Here are a few examples of merit scholarships that might be a great fit for you:

Coca-Cola Scholars Foundation
Financial Award: $20,000

According to the Foundation's website, www.coca-colascholarsfoundation.org, "Coca-Cola provides scholarships to students based on their academic records, volunteer work, and leadership skills. All applicants must plan to attend an accredited college in the U.S."

Gates Millennium Scholars Program
Financial Award: Varies

According to the Foundation's website, www.gmsp.org,
Bill and Melinda Gates started the Gates Millennium Scholars Program for "outstanding minority students with

significant financial need." The scholarships are for students interested in disciplines such as computer science, engineering, and mathematics. If any of these scholars want to continue to graduate school, they are awarded scholarships for that, as well. The award is renewable, and the amount varies based on need.

Foot Locker Scholarship
Financial Award: $20,000, dispersed as $5,000 per year

www.footlockerscholarathletes.com, says, "Foot Locker offers a four-year scholarship for students that demonstrate excellence in school, on their sports team and in their communities. The award amount is $20,000 spread out over four years. The award is only for high school seniors who want to attend a four-year college."

Do you have a gift or talent that you can use to help you secure a merit scholarship? List some of your gifts and talents here, then do some research to see if there are any merit scholarships that match what you have to offer.

_____

_____

_____

_____

8.

Test Me

Anyone here a big fan of taking tests? Well, whether you're a fan or not, every single day you're faced with various tests that can either make you, break you, or build you. It's all in your perspective. In this chapter, however, we're going to talk about tests that can pay you, or better stated, tests that can pay for your education. Now, I'm pretty sure you've either heard of these tests, taken these tests, or you're getting prepared to sit for them, and I want you to know all the benefits tied to your studying and investing your time so that you can excel and get the scores you need to help position yourself to get help with paying for college.

Look at all the information I found on www.nationalmerit.org:

What is it? "The *National Merit Scholarship Program** is an academic competition for recognition and college scholarships that began in 1955. United States high school students enter the National Merit Scholarship Program by taking the **Preliminary SAT/National Merit Scholarship Qualifying Test (PSAT/NMSQT®)**, which serves as an initial screen of over 1.5 million entrants each year, and by meeting published program entry and participation requirements."

How do I qualify for it?
1. take the PSAT/NMSQT in the specified year of the high school program, and no later than the third year in

49

grades 9 through 12, regardless of grade classification or educational pattern;

2. be enrolled as a high school student (traditional or homeschooled), progressing normally toward graduation or completion of high school, and planning to accept admission to college no later than the Fall following completion of high school; and

3. attend high school in the United States, the District of Columbia, or U.S. commonwealth and territory; or meet the citizenship requirements for students attending high school outside the United States."

Program Recognition

"Of the 1.5 million entrants, some 50,000 with the highest PSAT/NMSQT® Selection Index scores (calculated by doubling the sum of the Reading, Writing and Language, and Math Test scores) qualify for recognition in the National Merit Scholarship Program. In September, these high scorers are notified through their schools that they have qualified as either Commended Students or Semifinalists."

Commended Students

"In late September, more than two-thirds (about 34,000) of the approximately 50,000 high scorers on the PSAT/NMSQT receive Letters of Commendation in recognition of their outstanding academic promise. Commended Students are named based on a nationally applied Selection Index score that may vary from year to year, and is typically below the level required for participants to be named Semifinalists in their respective states. Although Commended Students do not continue in the competition for National Merit Scholarships, some of these students do become candidates for Special Scholarships sponsored by corporations and businesses."

Semifinalists

"In early September, about 16,000 students, or approximately one-third of the 50,000 high scorers, are notified that they have qualified as Semifinalists. To ensure that academically talented young people from all parts of the United States are included in this talent pool, Semifinalists are designated on a state-representational basis. Semifinalists are the highest scoring entrants in each state. Qualifying scores vary from state to state and from year to year, but the scores of all Semifinalists are extremely high. NMSC provides scholarship application materials to Semifinalists through their high schools. To be considered for a National Merit Scholarship, Semifinalists must advance to Finalist standing in the competition by meeting high academic standards and all other requirements explained in the information provided to each Semifinalist. View the Requirements and Instructions for Semifinalists in the 2021 National Merit Scholarship Program for more information about what Semifinalists must do. (Adobe Acrobat Reader is required.)"

Finalists

"In February, some 15,000 Semifinalists are notified that they have advanced to Finalist standing. High school principals are also notified and provided with a Certificate of Merit to present to each Finalist."

Winner Selection

"All winners of Merit Scholarship awards (Merit Scholar®
designees) are chosen from the Finalist group based on their
abilities, skills, and accomplishments—without regard to
gender, race, ethnic origin, or religious preference. A variety of
information is available for NMSC to evaluate: The Finalist's
academic record, information about the school's curriculum
and grading system, the PSAT/NMSQT Selection Index score,
the high school official's written recommendation, information
about the student's activities and leadership, and the Finalist's
own essay."

What do I earn? Types of Merit Scholarship Awards

"Beginning in March and continuing to mid-June, NMSC
notifies approximately 7,600 Finalists that they have been selected
to receive a Merit Scholarship® award. Merit Scholarship awards
are of three types:

National Merit® $2500 Scholarships

Every Finalist competes for these single-payment
scholarships, which are awarded on a state-representational
basis. Winners are selected by a committee of college admission
officers and high school counselors without consideration of
family financial circumstances, college choices, or majors and
career plans.

Corporate-sponsored Merit Scholarship awards

Corporate sponsors designate their awards for children of
their employees or members, for residents of a community where
a company has operations, or for Finalists with career plans the

sponsor wishes to encourage. These scholarships may either be renewable for four years of undergraduate study or be one-time awards.

College-sponsored Merit Scholarship awards

Officials of each sponsor college select winners of their awards from Finalists who have been accepted for admission and have informed NMSC by the published deadlines that the sponsor college or university is their first choice. These awards are renewable for up to four years of undergraduate study. The published deadlines for reporting a sponsor college as first choice can be viewed on page 4 of the Requirements and Instructions semifinalists in the 2021 National Merit® Scholarship Program."

Look at the information I also found on www.act.org:

What is it? "*The ACT® test motivates students to perform to their best ability. Test scores reflect what students have learned throughout high school and provide colleges and universities with excellent information for recruiting, advising, placement, and retention."

Who can take it? "The ACT test is designed for the tenth, eleventh, and/or twelfth grade levels, to provide schools and districts with the data necessary to position students for success after high school."

What are you being tested on? "The ACT contains four multiple-choice tests—English, mathematics, reading, and science—and an optional writing test. These tests are designed to measure skills that are most important for success in post-secondary education and that are acquired in secondary education. The score range for each of the four multiple-choice tests is 1–36. The Composite score is the average of the four test scores rounded to the nearest whole number."

What do I earn? "There are several colleges that give scholarships based on SAT/ACT scores, as well as additional qualifiers like your GPA or class rank."

What is it? *The CLEP: https://clep.collegeboard.org/about-clep/key-exam-information

According to collegeboard.org, "This rigorous program allows students from a wide range of ages and backgrounds to demonstrate their mastery of introductory college-level material and earn college credit. Students can earn credit for what they already know by getting qualifying scores on any of the exams being offered."

What do I earn? College credit!!!!!! Not only do students who earn credit through CLEP have better academic outcomes than their non-CLEP counterparts, but they also increase their likelihood of degree completion.

Break it down more: "You can study for it or you can be ready for it naturally due to your previous education and knowledge of the topic, but the CLEP is an exam you take through the College Board that allows you to show your proficiency in a specific subject matter. If you pass the test, that turns into a college credit. It's important, though, to make sure your specific college or university will accept the credit."

Prior Coursework

"Some colleges won't grant credit for a CLEP exam if you've already attempted a college-level course closely aligned with that exam. For example, if you successfully completed English 101 or a comparable course on another campus, you wouldn't receive CLEP credit in that same subject. Also, some colleges won't allow you to earn CLEP credit for a course that you failed."

*This data is from 2022

9.

Learn, Earn, and Pay with Tuition Remission

Remember how we talked about the employer tuition assistance program in Chapter 5? Well, what if I told you that there's actually opportunities where you can go to college, work for the college, get paid by the college, and the college will cover the cost of most or all of your tuition? This, my friend, is what we call tuition remission. It's almost like the perfect scenario. You learn, earn, and pay for college. That's what I call a triple win.

So, what does this look like for you? Well, if you snag yourself a job at a college or university that offers this benefit, then you could use this avenue as a way to pay for college and reduce your need for student loans. But, before you run off and apply for a job at the college you want to attend, be sure to read and understand the requirements and eligibility factors in order for you to take advantage of this opportunity. Every school is different, so you want to be sure that you do your research before jumping in head first. Here are some things you might want to know.

- Many universities require full-time employees to work a certain amount of time before these tuition remission benefits apply to them, and a further period of time before the benefits are applied to their dependents.

- Some may require proof of financial need.

- Full-time employees may not be able to register as full-time students.

You can start by looking up this information online, or you can contact the Human Resource Department of the college you are interested in working for and getting your degree.

Now, if your parent works at a college or university, you might want to talk to your parent or guardian to see if they qualify for this benefit as well. Tuition remission is a benefit that can also be handed down to an employee's child, and, of course, that varies from college to college, so do your research. It might not be the school you have your heart set on, but sometimes you have to put your "wants" to the side if you feel the "need" to live a debt-free life and graduate from college ready to save, earn, and grow your money versus paying back thousands of dollars in student loans.

Hear what Jessi has to say about how tuition remission not only helped her, but also helped her husband, too!

Rockell: Jessi, can you tell me a little bit more about the tuition remission program at your place of employment and what that looks like?

Jessi: I work for the University of Central Florida. How the tuition reimbursement or tuition waiver program works is that they'll pay up to six credit hours of undergraduate or graduate coursework. I have worked with UCF for about eleven years, and up until about five years ago, they only paid for the actual employee. About five years ago, they expanded the program to include spouses, and by that time, my husband already had an AA. This benefit was helpful when he transferred to UCF and his financial aid had kind of run out because, initially, he went to a for-profit school.

Rockell: It's great to hear that they expanded the program for spouses. So, if I was a freshman straight out of high school, and I got a job on campus outside of work-study, would I qualify, too?

Jessi: Yeah. As long as you work, because there are different types of employees.

Rockell: Okay. Awesome. And do you know how much it has saved you or your husband by taking advantage of this program?

Jessi: Yeah, I'd say probably about anywhere between like, twenty to thirty grand.

Rockell: That is so good! How can a senior in high school or an undergraduate student position themselves to get a job on campus so that they can take advantage of this benefit? What tips or suggestions would you say to that student to start doing now to better prepare themselves to qualify for a job on campus?

Jessi: Get their resume right. Because these are real jobs. They can possibly qualify for entry level positions like coordinators, secretaries, and program assistants. They usually all require a high school diploma, but they're still real jobs. A high school student would have to have a resume that is decent enough because a lot of people really want to get into UCF, seeing that the benefits are spectacular on top of just the free tuition, and make connections with a lot of people, like managers of different departments with hiring capabilities. Another great thing to do would be to start making connections with people at the fairs, like even admissions and financial aid, and their staff who come out to do these fairs—make connections with them. You can say something like, "Hey, are you guys hiring for a program assistant or a receptionist, or a front desk person."

Rockell: I love it. That's so on point. So, start building your resume as early as possible. You can do that in high school if you're working. Do your research, look at what job opportunities already exist, and start making those connections at the fairs. Does that sound accurate?

Jessi: Right. Right.

Rockell: That's perfect. And would you consider this a good route to help pay for college?

Jessi: Definitely. My husband definitely would not have been able to pay for it had I not been working at UCF.

List your top five colleges, then do your research. Do they offer tuition remission? What are the eligibility requirements?

_____

_____

_____

_____

_____

_____

_____

10.

The Side Hustle

The Airheads and Ring-Pops cost twenty-five cents each, and the Blow-Pops were seventy-five cents; I mean, they came with the gum-filled center, so you can understand the value in that, right? I thought it was worth the extra quarter, and so did many of my clients, who were my fifth-grade friends and their siblings. The exchange of money was swift and flawless. I eventually started making keychains out of lanyard plastic string, and those were a hit. I had a side hustle before I even knew what it was. In fifth grade, it dawned on me that there was an opportunity to make money and I was going to seize the moment. Were students allowed to sell things on school grounds? Probably not, but my fifth grade self was willing to shoot the shot and see what happened.

Let me ask, have you ever had a side-hustle? Do you currently have a side hustle? Why did you start your side hustle? It probably has something to do with making money, and maybe you're doing something you actually enjoy, which is great! So, if you're a college-bound student or even an undergraduate student and you have a side-hustle, this can be an effective way to put some money aside and save for college. I don't care if you only save a couple hundred dollars, it all adds up and every single penny counts. Plus, you're learning what it looks like to save your money and delay gratification. Friends, you're learning a skill that many adults still have not learned and implemented. If you have a side-hustle, that means you're taking extra time out of your life to produce a product or provide a service. Your side-hustle money should always have a goal and a why? Why am I working extra hard to make this money? What is the goal of having this money? If you're a student, you can say that your goal is to save some of this money to fund your college education or pay for your books and other college expenses that might come up.

If you're thinking about starting a side-hustle, here are a few things you should keep in mind before you move forward:

1. Your academics are the main focus, and if you struggle with time management, then a side-hustle might not be a good fit. You need to be able to balance and manage your time so your grades and family life don't suffer. If you have support and can learn to manage your time effectively, then you might be good to go.

2. Do your research and see what other young people are doing; maybe there's something you're already interested in, but you should still do your research before you start buying products or offering your services to friends, family, and through social media.

3. Don't start alone. Seek out guidance from your parent, guardian, family member, mentor, coach, or anyone that you trust to give you advice and guidance. When you seek out the proper wisdom, people can help you to avoid mistakes, and this helps to speed up your success process.

4. Open a bank account. Get your parents or guardian to help you with this if you are not of the age to open a bank account.

I would encourage you to also open the account with your local credit union, especially if they offer scholarships to their members. Plus, credit unions usually have great interest rates, so when you're ready to look into getting your car, a credit card, or any other financial services, you already have a relationship with your credit union. Make sure that you're saving money. Put it in your account and let it continue to sit there until you're in college and you're ready to use that hard-earned money for college expenses.

Your side-hustle can help you pay for college or college expenses if you play your cards right.

List five side-hustle ideas you'd consider pursuing. What would you need to do to manage your time so that your side-hustle doesn't interfere with your academics?

_____

_____

_____

_____

_____

_____

11.

Programs That Pay

What's better than getting a free education and scholarships? Getting a free education, scholarships, and being a part of a program to help you thrive and succeed in college and your career! Believe it or not, there are programs and opportunities for you to receive academic support and the resources you need to afford your college education and minimize your need for student loans.

Here are just a few of these amazing opportunities:**www.possefoundation.org**

*Posse: "The Posse Foundation identifies, recruits, and trains individuals with extraordinary leadership potential. Posse Scholars receive full-tuition leadership scholarships from Posse's partner colleges and universities."

Eligibility: Posse seeks students who are:

- Leaders in their high schools and communities.
- Committed to their education, and those who demonstrate academic potential.
- Interested in teamwork and diversity.
- Positive, motivated, talented, and ambitious young people"

www.questbridge.org

*QuestBridge: "QuestBridge is a powerful platform that connects the nation's brightest students from low-income backgrounds with leading institutions of higher education and further opportunities. 'We are an aggregator of excellence.' By facilitating these exchanges, QuestBridge aims to increase the percentage of talented low-income students attending the nation's best universities and the ranks of national leadership itself."

Eligibility: "QuestBridge is looking for high school seniors who have shown outstanding academic ability despite financial challenges. 'We take a holistic approach to reviewing applications, and we do not have absolute criteria or cut-offs for GPA, standardized test scores, income, or other factors.'"

QuestBridge Graduate School Match: "Applying to MBA programs through the QuestBridge Graduate School Match is unique from other MBA application processes because you can be considered for admission and a full-tuition scholarship through a non-binding Match round."

www.sasdreamfactory.org

*School For Advanced Studies: "School for Advanced Studies (SAS) is a nationally recognized collegiate high school of excellence, a combined effort between Miami-Dade County Public Schools (MDCPS) and Miami Dade College (MDC). Students attending SAS complete their last two years of high school (11th and 12th grade) while they obtain a two-year Associate in Arts degree from Miami Dade College. The opportunity for acceleration and enrichment attracts motivated and academically talented students. SAS takes pride in its diverse student population, nurturing learning environment, and commitment in providing all students with a rich and rigorous liberal arts education, with many of its students specializing in STEM. School for Advanced Studies provides a uniquely supportive transition between secondary and post-secondary education."

Eligibility: "A School for Advanced Studies application becomes available each fall for all public, charter, private, and homeschooled students who are currently in the tenth grade. SAS is not a magnet school. Student selection is based on completion of basic requirements for admission and a random ranking of qualified applicants up to the point where the enrollment cap is reached. When the number of eligible applicants exceeds the number of seats available, a random selection process will be utilized to admit eligible applicants. Annual enrollment is limited."

www.jkcf.org

*****Jack Kent Cooke Foundation:** "Provides scholarship programs designed to encourage and support outstanding students who work hard and have financial need. Our scholarships provide financial assistance and academic support to high school, undergraduate, and graduate students. In addition to the monetary award, students join a thriving network of nearly

3,000 Cooke Scholars."

Young Scholars Program: "The Cooke Young Scholars Program is a selective five-year, pre-college scholarship for high-performing 7th grade students with financial need. It provides comprehensive academic and college advising, as well as financial support for school, Cooke-sponsored summer programs, internships, and other learning enrichment opportunities."

College Scholarship Program: "The Cooke College Scholarship Program is an undergraduate scholarship program available to high-achieving high school seniors with financial need who seek to attend and graduate from the nation's best four-year colleges and universities."

Undergraduate Transfer Scholarship: "The Cooke Undergraduate Transfer Scholarship is a highly selective scholarship for the nation's top community college students seeking to complete their bachelor's degrees at four-year colleges or universities. Each Cooke Scholar has access to generous financial support for two to three years, college planning support, ongoing advising, and the opportunity to connect with the thriving community of fellow Scholars."

Along with the amazing opportunities listed above, fellowships are also programs that vary in scholarship and educational benefits. Many fellowships can be found for graduate students looking to further their knowledge and experience with a specific topic.

Fellowships

What is a fellowship? According to collegeraptor.com, "A fellowship can refer to several different programs. The type of program that the fellowship program is depends on the fellow's field of study. The organization hosting the fellowship could require the student to study a specific topic outside of school, work to bolster and help the local community, or do research. They are generally for graduate students who are looking for learning opportunities and extra experience. They can last anywhere between two months to two years.

In exchange for the students' work, they can receive funding for their research as well as for their schooling. This can be anywhere from $5,000 to $50,000 with some living and travel expenses added on. The work completed can also be a great addition to a graduating student's resume. Some employers even hire the fellow after the work is completed.

In order to apply for a fellowship, you have to be pursuing your Master's or a Ph.D. full time. Students interested in trying for this should regularly display leadership, communication skills, good writing ability, and motivation. You need high grades and research experience. Include your transcripts, letters of recommendation, writing sample, resume, and an outline of your proposed research project in your application. When applying, make sure to check for the exact materials required."

*This data is from 2022

If you're interested in looking for a fellowship, start with your school. Many offer programs right within their walls. Online databases are also a great place to look.

With all these money-saving opportunities, I wanted to hear more about the process and the outcome. **I spoke to Sean Smith about his QuestBridge journey and Alejandra Ugalde about her School for Advanced Studies experience. Check out what they had to say.**

Rockell: Hi, Sean, can you tell me more about the QuestBridge program?

Sean: The QuestBridge program is a program designed for low income and high achieving students to help them get into one of the top forty-five colleges and universities in the country. It allows universities and colleges to take a much closer look at your application because of the specific circumstances that you're under. That's basically what the program is. It's a really great program.

Rockell: Awesome. This program, again, is for the low-income students, but they're driven? Their academics prove that they are willing to come to the campus and put in the work, right?

Sean: Yes. Right.

Rockell: So how did you find out you were accepted and what school will you be attending?

Sean: I have a video. We were in the library, me and my friends, and I got an email saying that I should go check my application, because it's been updated. I went and checked it. I was so nervous. We just started jumping and screaming in the school library. I got accepted to Duke University!

Rockell: Wooooow! Congrats, Sean! When did you find out about this program? How did you find out about it?

Sean: I initially found out about QuestBridge, I think, I'm going to say, my sophomore year of high school. That's like 2019, maybe. I found out about it and I saw the massive list of colleges that they're partnering with, and instantly, I was drawn to it when I saw Stanford, Princeton, Yale, and other schools of that caliber. I thought, "I'm interested in this." I started building my list of colleges I was going to apply to in sophomore year, and I had specifically marked colleges that were partnering with QuestBridge, so I knew I could apply to those schools through QuestBridge. Actually, senior year, it slipped my mind just a tad bit, and a teacher came up to me because she thought I would be the perfect fit for this scholarship, and I'm so grateful to her, Ms. Monica Kirkman, amazing teacher. She reminded me about it, and basically, if she had never said anything about it to me, I highly doubt I would've remembered to apply to QuestBridge. I'm glad she did because I actually followed through with it and applied.

Rockell: I love how you said that you started already in sophomore year, thinking about the schools, creating your list, and that sounds strategic to me. Like, if these are the schools that they're partnering with, let me see if any of these schools already match the kind of school I'm looking for. Also, kudos to Ms. Kirkman for reminding you. She must have been like, "Hey, don't you forget." That seat was waiting for you, Sean. All you had to do was shoot your shot and apply.

Sean: Right.

Rockell: Why did you apply? What was it that drew you to this program?

Sean: I knew I met the qualifications. I am a low-income student and I am a high achiever, but I say that humbly. I happened to have earned a lot of positions and a lot of titles, and I do the best with those titles. I serve, and I make it so much more than just a title, but I use it to serve other people and do what I'm supposed to do with said position. With that, I knew that I met the criteria and that this was a program that I should apply for.

Rockell: That's great. What drew you to QuestBridge? What is it that attracted you to it?

Sean: I will have to say the colleges attracted me to it, because those are such ... how do I want to phrase it? Those colleges are huge. They're a big deal. It takes a lot of courage to even think about applying to one of those colleges, let alone actually applying and then actually getting in. I thought that this program was what I needed to get to where I needed to go.

Rockell: Love it. Is there a scholarship piece attached to this program?

Sean: Yes. I received a full-ride scholarship, and that encompasses everything, room and board, tuition, meal plans. I believe they also cover travel expenses as well in certain cases. I know this is probably one of your other questions you're asking, but I'm saving well over $300,000 because of this scholarship.

Rockell: Dude!!! You say that, and that gives me goosebumps. That is crazy good.

Sean: It is.

Rockell: Oh, my goodness. I'm so happy for you. What can students do to position themselves to qualify for a program like QuestBridge or similar? What are some of the things you would say to that student who's reading this right now and is excited about your story to start doing so they can position themselves to follow in your footsteps?

Sean: The two main criteria, once again, are low income and high achieving students. Of course, not everybody is low income. Some people are sort of in the middle. Some people are on the higher end of that. But QuestBridge can be a bit flexible, so if you think you are sort of in the middle, then I do definitely encourage still apply because based on your academics and your extracurriculars, you may still be what QuestBridge is looking for. When it comes to being a high-achieving student, as a national officer and a state officer for FBLA, every time I visit members and I visit chapters and I talk to people, I tell them the same thing, and that is to take any opportunity that you can. It's all about taking in those opportunities and having some sort of will to not only just take the opportunity, but to grow into it, learn something from it. Whether you think, "I just don't want to do this, or this is not for me, or this is something that I want to continue" and you believe you can see yourself on a path to this after high school, throughout high school, or whatever it may be, I think taking those opportunities is going to allow you to go somewhere, give you a path, and help you figure out what it is that you want to do.

Rockell: That is perfect. Taking advantage of opportunities. I feel like more opportunities lead to more opportunities. I love what you said about your titles. You don't just wear the title to wear the title, but it's like a badge of honor. You serve as a member of FBLA, and I'm pretty sure when you get on campus, you're still going to have that serving mentality. I'm so excited to see your journey.

Rockell: If it wasn't for the QuestBridge program and scholarship, how were you going to pay for college? What was that picture looking like for you?

Sean: In addition to my massive list of colleges, I knew I was going to apply to a pretty decent-sized list of outside scholarships. I was actually looking into many other scholarships besides QuestBridge. I was looking into the Jackie Robinson Scholarship and some local scholarships as well. I think people also tend to miss out on local scholarships. I was going to apply to my local National Panhellenic Fraternity and Sororities, their alumni chapters, and the scholarships they offer. I just had a nice list of outside scholarships I knew I would apply to in case QuestBridge didn't work out.

Wow! Isn't Sean's journey amazing? He's definitely saving money and staying far away from student loans. Alejandra did things a little differently, but it led her to save a ton of money on college.

Rockell: Alejandra, what is the SAS program in your opinion?

Alejandra: In simple words, SAS is a full-time, dual enrollment program that lasts for two years of high school. So, students attend SAS and complete eleventh and twelfth grades at one of five different Miami Dade College campuses and simultaneously obtain a two-year associate and arts degree from Miami Dade College.

Rockell: Nice, so when did you find out about the program?

Alejandra: So, I first heard about SAS when I was in middle school, actually. I was an eighth grader at Ammons Middle School, and they were hosting a high school fair, where they had invited parents to come. It was a midday event, so around 10:00 AM to 12:00 PM it lasted. It was similar to a career fair where you have different high schools come out, present their programs, and share different opportunities. I was listening to more notable schools like Coral Reef and Ferguson. These are traditional schools that are more of a common household name.

SAS was out there, too, as Mr. Dennis Lindsay mentioned, his opening line, which I still remember to this day, was, "Who loves free college?" And that resonated with me because I thought, "Hey, free college. Sign me up for sure."

Rockell: So why did you apply for this program?

Alejandra: I applied for many different reasons, but I believe the core reason why I applied was because I wanted to be a bit more challenged. Terra was my original high school that I was in attendance at. It was a great environment. I made great friends, had quality teachers, but a part of me just felt like there's something else I could be doing. This is regular high school, extracurriculars, being on the soccer team, getting good grades. But I thought, "Is there something more I could be doing with my time?" Because I would hear of other people already applying for scholarships, already taking Dual-Enrollment courses. I'm like, "How do I get into that?"

Rockell: Look at you challenging yourself! Are there any other reasons you applied?

Alejandra: Yeah. So, upon actually filling out my subject selection form for my junior year, during my sophomore year at Terra, my counselor at the time had advised me that it would not be wise to take more than two AP courses. Being the overachiever that I am, I had actually signed up for five. And they were quick to say, "Maybe don't do that. We don't want you to be too stressed out with SATs, and we know you're on the girls' soccer team and the course load from taking many

APs." So that, to me, wasn't really the push or the motivation that I needed or wanted in order to take on more. I was like, "Hey, I can do this. Give me more. I can take on more on my plate."

Rockell: Wow! You were ready. So how has being a participant in the SAS program impacted you?

Alejandra: I would say financially and being able to experience and take a variety of different collegiate-level courses while still trying to figure out what my path was in life, whether that was pre-med, so I needed to be STEM related, or if it was to be a teacher, then I needed to take an educational path. There are so many different majors nowadays that you can choose from, but it's great that I was able to take classes that surround these different majors and still accrue credits that contribute to my associate in arts. On top of that, financially, it definitely saved my parents and myself tons of money.

Alejandra: I guess the third reason would be that it also impacted me to join the workforce at an early age, because I know a lot of kids, maybe in high school, want a job and are looking to join, I don't know, retail or a chain store, like Publix or Walmart, something just to get their foot in the door, but I was able to take on a data coordinator position at a private research facility. Not many recent high school graduates get those opportunities, since you're a recent high school grad. What experience do you have? What was your education like? So, you can only fill up your resume so much. But because I had propelled myself into that challenging program, graduated, done well, and came out with an AA degree and a high school degree at the age of eighteen, I was more than qualified for the position, even at entry level. I was definitely able to handle all the responsibilities that came with that position.

Rockell: What can students do now to position themselves for a program like SAS or something similar in your opinion?

Alejandra: I would definitely focus on strengthening that GPA, because it really might seem like, "Okay, getting a few Bs, getting a few Cs here, it won't really matter in the end." But it does. I didn't think about it at the time, but I actually didn't do as well in my freshman year and actually came out with a "C" and a "D" in math and science, because I struggled a lot. Sophomore year, I turned that up because, thinking back about SAS, I knew the requirements that they had in place. I said, "Okay, if I really want to challenge myself, I need to show that I can come back from missteps." And so, I definitely strengthened my GPA. I was always trying from there on out, and just being balanced in life—throughout education, but also socially and personally. Having extracurriculars is great, because I understand school can't be everything sometimes, even though it is for some people, which is totally fine. But it's great to have that balance, because it sets you apart from the rest. What else do you do besides academics? You can excel surpassingly in academics, but do you play any sports? Are you in any clubs? Are you part of student government? Things like that, I joined early on. So, from eighth grade, I was already in sports, Spanish Club, English Honors Club, Math Club. So, coming into sophomore year, I continued the sports, kind of left some of the clubs. Then, going into sophomore year, I realized, "Okay, you got to kind of clean up." So, I did Future Business Leaders of America, came back to Spanish Honors Club, and it really kind of sharpened my well-roundedness.

Rockell: I like how you were able to reflect and adjust when it came to your grades and extracurricular activities. Let me ask, because you said that freshman year you had some low grades. So, sophomore year, you had to pick it up. What did you do in order to pick up your grades, or did it just happen easily for you? Was there anything special you did?

Alejandra: So, for me, I had to sacrifice being in a sports club. So, I played soccer, I want to say, for my first quarter up until probably October, I want to say. But I knew that wasn't going to be enough. I really needed to make a drastic change in order to up my grades and just give myself more time to study. Because when you're on a club team or a recreational team, it takes hours and hours away from your day. I knew if I wanted to excel in one area, I had to sacrifice in another. In the long run, I knew it would pay off. So, I took that step back from soccer and I really focused on just studying for more hours a day than what I was getting before.

Rockell: Did you do any tutoring or was it just more self-studying?

Alejandra: Definitely, I was always the kid who was afraid to ask for help. I started going to tutoring hours after school, working with my teachers that I was struggling with. It's easy for me to say, "Oh, I don't get this." But maybe someone else can say, "Hey, maybe you don't get this because of this." So definitely working with tutors and the after-school tutoring hours with them.

Rockell: That's great. How much money would you say that you and your family saved by you being in the SAS program?

Alejandra: I want to say roughly about $ 10,000, give or take. I was looking up at Miami Dade their cost per credit right now, and it's about $ 118 with tuition and fees. So, doing the math, I was at Miami Dade for five semesters and I took anywhere from 9 to 15 credits. I wasn't full time, because since you're first starting Dual-Enrollment, they don't throw you into the wolves and say, "Hey, here's the twelve-credit course load. Enjoy. Plus, high school coursework." So, it was very manageable at first. And then in the summer, I took on more. And then senior year, I knew, "Okay, I can balance both. Let me take on more." So, in total, I would say about $ 10,000 plus or minus, but that includes all the tuition, all the cost of books. Books, if you know, from any school really, can range from a hundred to up to $500. There were laboratory fees, because I was taking biology and anatomy. Online programs, because every course is different. Some might just use paper and pen, and take home worksheets. Or others use online programs, which can cost up to two or three hundred dollars. And then, of course, you have materials. I saved a lot!

12.

Crowdfunding For Education

When I was a kid, I had no problem asking relatives and loved ones for money. Really, I had no shame in my game. Of course, I always used my manners, especially if I knew my semi-rich uncle (at least that's what I thought he was) was stopping by my house. I had no problem asking for ten, fifteen, or twenty dollars. Now hear me out, I didn't just open my hand, smile, and say, "Can I please have ten dollars". No way, if that was the case, I'd probably get shut down half the time. Instead, I had a reason or a story to accompany me asking for money. So instead, I smiled and said, "My school is having a book fair this week and I'd love to buy a new book to read; can I please have ten dollars?" And most of the time, because I had a reason or a story, the answer was yes.

Somehow, as an adult, it doesn't really work anymore, maybe because I don't have that cute school girl smile or maybe it's because my requests go way beyond the ten dollars for the book store (insert emoji with palms up and shoulders shrugged). Who knows? But as a student, you can ask for money and you'd be surprised by the number of people that say yes and are willing to support you. Of course, just like it mattered when I was in elementary school, it still matters today. You must have an honest story, be humble, and ditch the shame of asking someone for their hard-earned money. This is what crowdfunding for your education is all about. It's an opportunity for you to ask loved ones and strangers to support you on your college journey. Most people understand the financial burdens that are tied to earning a degree, and most people will understand why you're crowdfunding to pay for school if you do a really good job of sharing your why. There will be some people who don't agree with this or have something negative to say. I think it's best if you just keep it moving... Don't allow the naysayers and negative people to stop you from pursuing your dreams without tagging on thousands of dollars in student loans. Every person, at some point in their life, will need to reach out for help especially after doing everything possible, which brings me to my next tip when it comes to crowdfunding for your education. Along with sharing your story, it's pretty crucial that you also share all the work you've already done to secure funding. That means you need to apply for FAFSA, numerous scholarships, and if you've saved money, let people know that when you create your crowdfunding page. The last thing a person wants to do is give money to a student who hasn't even tried to put in the work on their own. You have to show that you've been putting in the work, trying, and in the end, you still need some additional support. Also, don't forget that showing proof of your grades is a great way to show your supporters that you're not here to waste their money. Every penny will be put to good use.

If you think crowdfunding for your education might be a good option and you're not ashamed to ask for help, then shoot your shot.

Here's an example for inspiration, or you can always head over to the GoFundMe website to see what other students are sharing.

 Nicole Smith is organizing this fundraiser.

"Have you ever worked so hard on a project only to get to the end and realize that you don't have enough resources to complete it? That's the journey I'm on. My name is Nicole Smith, and I'm on a four-year journey to complete the project of earning my bachelor's degree in political science. This project is near and dear to my heart because it's going to allow me to create change in communities that need it the most and be a voice for those who can't speak. I've been diligently working on this project and earning grades that display my work ethic. I've secured several scholarships and awards that have gotten me this far but due to a financial crisis, I have found myself with very little resources and money to complete this journey. I can't begin to explain how your support and contribution will not only impact my life, but it will reflect in the lives of the people I lead, serve, and advocate for over the course of my career."

13.

Be All That You Can Be with A Debt Free Degree

"**B**e All You Can Be" served as the Army slogan from 1980 to 2001. Even though that is no longer the slogan for the Army, I think you can still be all you can be while serving your country and earning a degree with little to no student loan debt. Now I know the military isn't for everyone, so I don't want you to consider this as an option to pay for school unless you are really interested in joining the military and all it has to offer. This career path is an important one, so doing your research and connecting with others that are serving or have served in the military is a great idea. Ask questions so you have a better vision of what you can possibly expect on your journey. I have quite a few friends and family members that have joined the military or retired, and some of them have already taken advantage of the tuition assistance program or the G.I. Bill that is offered.

My classmate that I graduated from high school with gave me the inside scoop on how he earned a debt-free degree while serving in the Army. Check it out:

Rockell: How has the military helped you pay for college?

Uwan: So, the program that I've taken advantage of the most is TA. Tuition Assistance will cover the cost of the class, but it will not cover your books. You do have to be currently serving on Active Duty or Active Reserve to take advantage of Tuition Assistance. TA will cover $250 per semester credit hour. If you happen to attend a private school that charges more than the standard rate, you may have to cover the rest out of your own pocket. I went to Embry-Riddle, which at the time was charging approximately $350 per credit hour, so I had to pay the difference. I was also able to find used books online at a very affordable price.

Rockell: Perfect, and how much was the Tuition Assistance? Is it a semester? Is it a year? What does the number look like?

Uwan: So, every year, TA benefits change as the defense budget is reallocated. While I was using the program, I was allowed to complete 12-18 semester credit hours. Currently, for fiscal year 2022, Sailors are allowed to take eighteen college credits and a maximum of $4,500 annually.

Rockell: Got you. Were all of your college expenses covered, which I think you answered, not technically, because you had to pay out of pocket for your books, is that right?

Uwan: If I chose to use my GI Bill benefits, everything would've been covered because the GI Bill will pay for your class, your books, and pay you a housing allowance. All right. This is the part that I want you to be able to capture. So, with Tuition Assistance, I can only use it while I'm on active duty. I can no longer use TA once I leave the military. However, with my GI bill, I have the option to use while on active duty or once I leave the military. The GI Bill can also be transferred to dependents such as my spouse or children. The smart thing to do is to take maximum advantage of Tuition Assistance while on active duty to earn your degree, then transfer your GI bill to a dependent. It's possible to pay for two degrees with one enlistment. Also, the GI Bill will only cover thirty-six months of school, but there is a way to extend it for an additional twelve months, so it's enough to cover a four-year degree. In my situation, if I started using my GI Bill, I would've used it all and I wouldn't have anything to give to my son.

Rockell: That's a smart move. And I'm just going to restate that just to make sure I understand. It's better to use the Tuition Assistance when you're on active duty, because once you're no longer active, you can't tap into the TA. Does that make sense?

Uwan: Correct.

Rockell: Well, let me ask you, so you were saying that some people tap into their TA and then they use their GI bill, so are you saying that some people even end up getting their bachelors and their masters because they max out everything? Are there restrictions around this? Or you can get whatever degree you want?

Uwan: You can get whatever degree you want and attend whatever school you want, as long as you can accomplish that outside of your normal duty hours. TA resets every single year, so you can continue your education as long as you don't go past the annual semester credit hours limit. That allows active-duty members to complete up to their masters if they wanted. It also has an annual cap, meaning the maximum budget is allocated at the beginning of each fiscal year. There've been several years throughout my long career where the annual budget was reached before the end of the fiscal year. In situations like this, Sailors would have the option to tap into their GI Bill benefits or wait until the start of the new fiscal year to continue their education.

Rockell: So, if you don't use it, you lose it?

Uwan: Pretty much, the Navy allocates a set amount of funds each year for TA. If the funds are not used, then they're reallocated to other programs the following year. Also, another benefit that's rarely talked about is how Sailors receive college credits for military training without ever stepping foot in a college classroom. For example, Sailors will earn nine college credits just for completing Basic Training (bootcamp). They'll also earn college credits from their "A" school, which is our technical training school for our specific career field. The number of credits in their A school varies depending on the career field.

Rockell: Wow, okay. Nine college credits, basic training. Love it. So, being in the military allows you to earn college credits through your training before you even step foot on campus?

Uwan: Correct, but I don't want to mislead you either. There's a caveat to that. Most of the credits are going to apply towards a degree that matches your career field in the Navy. For example, I joined the Navy as an aviation mechanic. An aviation university like Embry Riddle was able to accept 90 percent of my military credits. My military credits covered all my elective classes as well as a ton of my core curriculum because it was an aviation degree. If I were to take those same credits and apply them to a nursing program, odds are only my elective would have been covered, which is still not a bad deal.

Rockell: Got it. What advice would you give to students that are considering this path to pay for college?

Uwan: Do as much research as possible on all the different programs and career fields that we have to offer. So, there's actually four main paths to paying for college. I would want people to do research on Tuition Assistance, GI Bill, STA-21 program (Seaman to Admiral), and the Navy's NROTC program. In my opinion, these are the most common paths towards earning a college degree with little to no expense out of your own pocket. After you've done all your research, contact your local recruiter.

14.

You Can Save Something

Mema (that's my grandma) always spoke to me about saving money. She would always emphasize the need to save for a rainy day, whatever that means, says my ten-year-old self, but a rainy day today means college. I get it though; she was just trying to teach me about the importance of saving and helping me to develop that muscle so I wouldn't walk into adulthood not having the basic understanding of what it looks like to save, what it feels like to save and why I should save. Who in your family talks to you about saving money? Have you started saving yet? Where do you save your money? I know some students might say they can't save because they don't have a job or consistent income, and that's a fair argument, but I want to share how you can start saving even if you don't have a job, because the hardest part about saving is, well, saving.

Let's start saving!

1. Don't have a job? Neither did I until I was a junior in high school. Do you ever get money for your birthday, holidays, special occasions, or chores? If you answered yes, then you have the power to start developing that muscle to save. Now I'm not saying to save the whole $50 bill Uncle Rufus just gave you for your birthday, but I'm saying to take a percentage of that (maybe 15-20 percent=$7-10) and save it. It's in your best interest to

save your money in an actual savings account or bank account that your parents can help you open if you are not old enough to do it on your own. You can also tuck it away in a jar or special place in your room. You basically want your money out of sight from you and others.

2. Earn it! You can find creative ways to earn money or get a job. I've heard of students earning money for babysitting, dog walking, tutoring, coaching, baking, mowing lawns, and doing hair. I mean, the list goes on. I know several adults doing the same things I just shared as a side hustle. If you're a student and you can manage your time so that your academics don't suffer, you can find a way to earn some money and save some money.

3. Having a bank account plays a major role in saving your money. For most banks, you need to be at least eighteen years of age to open your account. If you are under the age requirement, talk to your parent or guardian about helping you open your account. Let them know that you are saving for college and want to place your money in a savings account so that account can grow with the money you put in it every week or month. When you're ready to register for classes or pay for books, that money will be there to help you. It doesn't matter if you save $400 or $2,000; the truth is, every single penny counts and that money is going to help you in one way or the other. Also, I would consider opening a bank account with a local credit union. Many of them offer scholarships, and some of them have a requirement that you must be a member to apply.

15.

If You Have No Other Choice

Do you want to graduate from college with thousands of dollars in student loans?

Did you apply for the FAFSA?

Did you apply for scholarships?

Are you still applying for scholarships?

Did you qualify for Dual-Enrollment or participate?

Did you identify potential employers that offer tuition assistance?

Did you, or are you currently trying your best to achieve the grades that can position you to qualify for an academic merit scholarship?

Did you, or are you currently trying your best to excel in your sport, art, leadership role, or other extra-curricular activity to position yourself to qualify for a merit scholarship or other programs that pay?

Did you, or are you studying hard and possibly getting tutoring to pass the PSAT, ACT, or CLEP?

Did you identify a program that pays that might be beneficial to you now or in the future?

Have you looked into the military as an option if you're not sure about college right now?

Is crowdfunding something you're willing to do?

Have you saved as much money as possible to put toward your education?

The bottom line is, are you doing everything possible to pay for college and avoid student loan debt?

If your answer is yes and you're still falling short, I want to remind you to keep applying for scholarships and keep looking for other opportunities. I also want to let you know that student loans are still an option. It's an option that I would love for you to avoid, but I also understand that even with all the work you're doing to secure money to pay for school, it might not be enough. So, if you've done everything to pay for college but you still need help, let's look at some student loan options that you can consider if you absolutely have to.

According to www.studentaid.gov, subsidized and unsubsidized loans are federal student loans for eligible students to help cover the cost of higher education at a four-year college or university, community college, or trade, career, or technical school. The U.S. Department of Education offers eligible

students at participating schools Direct Subsidized Loans and
Direct Unsubsidized Loans.

Subsidized loans:

Who can get Direct Subsidized Loans?
"Direct Subsidized Loans are available to undergraduate
students with financial need."

How much can you borrow?
"Your school determines the amount you can borrow, and
the amount may not exceed your financial need."

Who will pay the interest?
"The U.S. Department of Education pays the interest on a
Direct Subsidized Loan

- while you're in school at least half-time,
- for the first six months after you leave school (referred to
  as a grace period*), and
- during a period of deferment (a postponement of loan
  payments)"

Unsubsidized loans

Who can get Direct Unsubsidized Loans?
"Direct Unsubsidized Loans are available to undergraduate
and graduate students; there is no requirement to demonstrate
financial need."

How much can you borrow?

"Your school determines the amount you can borrow based on your cost of attendance and other financial aid you receive."

Who will pay the interest?

"You are responsible for paying the interest on a Direct Unsubsidized Loan during all periods."

Sherry Allen with Smart Loan Solutions dropped some great advice for students that will be taking out student loans to pay for their education. Smart Loan Solutions is already offering borrowers, students, and colleges/universities assistance in managing their student loan debt. Sherry also assists individuals with getting out of default on their loans. I knew she would be a great person to offer guidance.

Feel free to contact Sherry if you have any questions at www. smartloansol.com or info@smartloansol.com

Rockell: Sherry, can you tell me a little bit more about Smart Loan Solutions?

Sherry: Smart Loan Solutions is all about helping students, borrowers, and higher education institutions navigate the student loan process. Some people may be at the very beginning, where they just want more information about student loans and how they operate. If you are already a borrower and you've graduated, you may want to ask yourself, "What would I have to pay back for these loans?" Or "Which payment option will be best for me? I don't know which one to choose." Some people ask about public service loan forgiveness. If you work for a nonprofit institution, then yeah, you can get that student loan forgiven and I can show you the steps to take to get that done.

Rockell: Awesome. Love it. Love it. What would you say are the pros and cons of student loans?

Sherry: Whew. If you asked me about all my student loans, I would be like, "They're cons." The pros, though, are that it's accessible to students who may not have any other options, who might not have any savings, or who are first-generation college students and their families don't know about college and don't have the funds to do so. So, it can be for those types of students. It can help build credit for someone who doesn't have any credit. But you got to pay it back on time, of course, and you have to read the terms before you borrow. Also, it just makes the student successful in the future if they graduate with a great career path and are able to pay them back without any problems.

Rockell: Absolutely. And what would you say are the cons?

Sherry: Oh, you have a big debt when you graduate college, and for some students, that's a sticker shock. They're like, "Wait a minute, I borrowed that much money?" And it's like, "Yeah. Were you not reading the award letters that you were signing or agreeing to?" Also, depending on the amount that the student borrows, it could be hard for them to make those payments and live comfortably, especially if they don't know about the multiple options for payment plans and what you can do with the loans. You could start off small and, as you keep growing in your career, you can make your payments a little bit larger.

Rockell: Right, I am that student that was in sticker shock after borrowing my loans.

Sherry: The worst thing that could ever happen is if you don't make any payments on your student loan at all, you could go into default. If you go into default, a plethora of things can happen, like your credit score significantly dropping, getting your wages garnished, and you could lose your professional license and sometimes your driver's license, depending on the state you live in.

Rockell: Wow! So where should a student start if they find themselves needing student loans to pay for school? What should step one, step, two, and step three be?

Sherry: First, assess if you really need it. Look at your award letter to find out what your balance is. If you and your parents can't afford to make those payments, or you don't have any savings saved up, the first thing to do is talk to the financial aid office. They will walk you through the steps of doing the entrance counseling, letting you know what you're borrowing and why you're borrowing it. I always tell some students, too, that if you want to just research them on your own, Google is really good. Just type in, "What is a student loan?" And it will break down what a student loan is, and what the terms and conditions are. If you've ever looked at a master promissory note, the words are really, really small at the bottom, so you never really know what you're signing your name to. So, it's good to go online and look at those terms and conditions to see if that would be feasible for you.

Rockell: Are there any other loans that students should consider outside of those that come through the FAFSA? Maybe at their bank or their credit union, what are your thoughts on that?

Sherry: Mm-hmm. Yeah, most times, you can get the loans from a credit union or from a bank, but for students that do choose to do that, they need to look at the percentage rate, find out if it's going to be variable, or if it's going to just stay the same. You don't want to get a loan at 1.1% and then, by the time you graduate, that loan is at 11%. You want to make sure it has a cap; it won't go over a certain amount. They also need to look at the repayment options. Do you have the options of the different payment plans versus the federal government loans? Do you have cancellation policies versus the government loans? And then most times, when you borrow from your credit union or from a bank like Chase, they don't have those options. So just be very careful and read everything, read, read, read, read everything, and then weigh out every option that you possibly can before taking the student loan from outside of the federal government.

Rockell: Perfect. So, if a student is considering taking a student loan outside of the federal government, I just want to make sure I'm getting it right; they should do a compare and contrast of what the percentage rate is, what the payback options are and just list those things to see which one's going to give them the most bang for their buck, is that right?

Sherry: Yes, ma'am.

16.

If You Don't Take Action,
This Could Be Your Story

This chapter is just a reality check. It's a gentle but harsh reminder of why it's important for us to plan and implement as many of the previous chapters as possible. Not every opportunity will be a good fit for you, but I'm pretty sure there are more than enough opportunities for you to take advantage of in this book. Do your research, ask for help, and implement it.

Sometimes it's hard to fully understand the urgency of things that aren't happening to us now or won't impact us for several years from now. My hope is that you don't wait for it to happen to you. Take a glimpse into the reality of what it'll be like when you don't **do everything possible to pay for college and minimize your need for student loans.**

I connected with several amazing, successful individuals who have or had student loan debt. Even though they may have reached their goals and are still working on many more, they all shared how student loans are something they rather not have had on their journey to success. Read their stories. If nothing else, I hope their stories inspire you to start doing the groundwork to pay for college and avoid as much student debt as possible.

#1 Kit Sluys

Rockell: Kit, what did you major in when you were in college?

Kit: For my undergraduate, I majored in studio art. My graduate degree is in clinical psychology. I have a doctorate in clinical psychology and work as a psychologist.

Rockell: So, what was your game plan to pay for college prior to going to college?

Kit: I didn't really have one! I figured I would work part-time as much as possible. For undergrad, I knew I could get some grants. For graduate school, I just kind of figured I would have loans. Everyone else who had the degree I wanted seemed to have loans, so it seemed normal and okay.

Rockell: Right, so did you need loans the entire time you were in college?

Kit: I mostly took out loans for my graduate program. There wasn't an option to do the program part-time, so working full-time didn't seem like an option to me. I had one classmate in that program that worked full-time, but her attention was really divided. I just didn't think I could do both, and I didn't want to. Even if I did work full-time, though, I would've needed loans for the tuition.

Rockell: How much did you end up owing?

Kit: Over $400,000!

Rockell: Wow!!! That's a lot of money. How would you do things differently?

Kit: Yeah, I would have worked more in a field that wasn't related to my major while still in school. The part-time work I did during school was Teacher Assisting and editing papers for students. That did not pay much at all! I should have worked as a server or something. Every extra dollar would've helped. I'm also not sure I would have pursued the same degree. Being a psychologist is stable work, but I feel unstable a lot when I think about how much money I still owe.

Rockell: How has having student loans impacted your life?

Kit-It has impacted my life a lot. It impacts financial decisions today. My husband and I don't want to buy a house where we live currently (in Oregon) because the houses are so expensive and we just don't want to have that much debt. It also impacts the decisions I make regarding my career. If I didn't have the loans, I would have a lot more freedom in my work. As an example, I initially started working for an organization where I could have potentially gotten Public Service Loan Forgiveness, but I decided I just didn't want to do something I didn't love for ten years, so now I'm paying them off on my own.

Rockell: Student loans can have such a long-term impact. How long did it take you to pay off your loans? Or are you still paying?

Kit: I'm only 5 years out of school, so I am definitely still paying.

Rockell: Kit, what is your advice to students trying to figure out how to afford college?

Kit: I would ask them if college is what they really need to make a decent living. If you want to be a professional, like a doctor or a lawyer, and absolutely need an advanced degree, then go for it. But take your time. Work and save for a few years before starting your program. Go part-time if you can and if it will allow you to work more, and live with family or roommates to save on rent. If you don't want to be a professional, I would really consider what you can accomplish with a two-year degree and/or vocational school. Education is important for reasons other than income, but I think that should be pursued when you have the financial means, you know? You can always go back to school. You don't have to have things figured out right away. I wish I had worked more before getting my degree, and I started my graduate degree when I was twenty-seven. I would also recommend getting educated on finances and the power of saving money early. Listen to podcasts or read books on these topics. Take your time with school and save, save, save your money as early as you can! Avoid loans at all costs.

#2 Kayla Bradshaw

Rockell: Kayla, what did you major in?

Kayla: My first bachelor's was in human biology with a minor in biology. My second bachelor's was a bachelor of science in nursing.

Rockell: Are you currently working in the field in which you went to school for?

Kayla: The second degree, yes. Not the first degree. Maybe it was just a stepping stone, but I didn't need that.

Rockell: Got it, so when you were getting ready to go to college, what was your game plan to pay for college?

Kayla: Student loans. I didn't know anything else. I grew up in a rural community where we didn't really know about the resources. If our college prep counselors had the resources, I wasn't made aware of them. So yeah, I knew without a doubt that student loans would be the only way I could go to college.

Rockell: Did you apply for the FAFSA? Did you get anything from the FAFSA?

Kayla: So, I applied for the FAFSA and scholarships. I had $1,500 in scholarships. I think it was for two semesters' worth. And FAFSA, because my mom was a small business owner and it looked like she made money, but really, she didn't, we didn't get anything. Because of her business, she always filed late taxes, so I could never get the FAFSA filled out on time. So that's how it was for the first two years until I was able to get it to where I didn't have to be on her taxes anymore, or have her taxes on the FAFSA anymore. When I deployed to Iraq and came back, I didn't need to have her information anymore. I finally got financial assistance.

Rockell: Okay, so if you had an opportunity to go back, how would you have done things differently, knowing what you know about student loans?

Kayla: If the school didn't have the resources, I would've hired somebody to find me the scholarships to apply for. Now that I know that support exists, whether you pay a fee or do it for free, there are resources. I would most definitely have paid somebody to find me scholarships to apply for.

Rockell: You're right, support does exist. Do you recall how much in total you took out in student loans?

Kayla: I had a total of $80,000 in student loans.

Rockell: Was that for both of your degrees?

Kayla: Both of them. The first degree I think I had was about 25 or 30,000, and then I started getting assistance, so I didn't need the student loans, but the second degree was a second bachelor's. I was now married, so we didn't qualify for grants. I had already used up all of my GI Bill money, which when I went to school for the first time, the GI Bill did not pay out as much as it does now. The second degree - the one that I knew that I could actually start my career in - was where the rest of the student loans came from.

Rockell: Right, and fast forward to today, how would you say that student loans have impacted your life?

Kayla: It was always a burden when I finished the first degree and had to start paying back. I didn't have a job in my first degree because it was really just a stepping stone to med school, and I decided not to go to med school. So, I had to apply for income-driven payment plans, giving my pay stub as proof that I did not have the money to pay back the student loan payment they wanted me to pay. So, for many, many years, it was seventeen years in total that I had student loans for. We paid them off last year.

Rockell: Wow. That's awesome that you paid it off, but seventeen years is a long time to carry that loan.

Kayla: That's a long time. I could have done so much more with that 80,000. I could have invested a whole lot better with that 80,000 or slept better at night.

Rockell: Absolutely.

Kayla: Then my husband had student loans as well. He had $28,000 in student loans and because he's on active duty, the tuition reimbursement with active duty is very different. He took out student loans for 50 percent of his classes because they only paid for half of them. So, it was $108,000 of student loans plus whatever we paid in interest.

Kayla: That's a house.

Rockell: Sure is! When we don't know better, we don't do better, but yeah. What is your advice to students trying to figure out how to afford college, how to pay for college? What would you say to those students getting ready to transition into post-secondary education?

Kayla: Do everything you can to get a scholarship. Do everything you can to get a grant. Do work-study with the school. You can become a resident assistant and have your room, board, and meals paid for. You can do a lot of things if you just find the resources and are aware of it. I mean, awareness is the biggest factor in all of this. If you were like, loans are the only way you could go, if there were no grants, if there were no scholarships, then I guess student loans is what it is. But I feel like student loans are the worst thing that has come to this economy.

Rockell: Right. Right. And I tell students that it should literally be at the bottom of their list. First, maximize everything that you just stated, and then, at the end, if loans are all you have, then go for it, but still be smart about it.

Rockell: Are you a first-generation student and how will your kids pay for college if they choose to go?

Kayla: Yes, I am. We have four boys together. We have college accounts for them. We have the GI Bill split between two of them. We'll not allow them to take out student loans. I mean, if they end up being a rocket scientist and need eighty years of college, then I don't know what we'll do. But I do believe student loans are one of the worst things to happen to this economy. I don't ever want my kids to have to go through that. So, if we set aside even just a little bit every month for them now, we could make a huge difference. Whether they just need to borrow $5,000 in loans is okay, compared to $80,000.

Rockell: That sounds great!

#3 Michael Williams

Rockell: Michael, can you tell me, what did you major in when you went to college?

Michael: Well, I majored in electronics engineering when I first went in and upon completion of that, I went for my business administration degree.

Rockell: What was your game plan to pay for college prior to going to college?

Michael: I had no game plan going into it. I was more, I guess, my mindset as a teenager was that if they accepted me, I'd go, and then I'd figure it out later. The financial aid office told me I qualify and you know, all I have to pay back is $75 a month. So there really was no plan going into it.

Rockell: Okay, so it was a combination of FAFSA and figuring it out. So then why did you take out loans to pay for school?

Michael: At that point in my life, I didn't really have a plan. I know I liked electronic computers, and this was just that step of motion that I had to do after high school. Just further my education.

Rockell: Did you take out the loans for your bachelor's degree or master's? What did you take it out for specifically?

Michael: Yeah, the loan was for my associates and then my bachelor's. For the bachelor's, I was able to leverage an employer I was working with at the time, and they partially paid for it with some scholarships, but very small compared to the whole pie, but yeah, that was some financial assistance.

Rockell: Did you apply for any scholarships while you were in high school or in college?

Michael: No. No, that sounds so foreign, and that wasn't even a thought for me in high school.

Rockell: How much did you owe in student loans?

Michael: It was about $30,000. My first degree was, I guess, eighteen thousand, and then the other one was maybe five or six thousand because it was online classes, but then just with interest and penalties, it grew.

Rockell: So how would you do things differently, knowing what you know today. If you could go back and do things differently, what would you do?

Michael: Well, knowing what I know now, I realize there's a lot of free money out there. You just have to go look for it. I also know that there are a lot of organizations and charities as well, that are just dying to give money away to needy kids. It's just a matter of finding them and applying. That is knowledge and guidance I didn't have in high school.

Rockell: So, when you completed your FAFSA, did you receive any money at all, or was it just student loans?

Michael: I believe I got, like, maybe a little tiny, small Stafford loan. I don't know, a loan of twelve hundred or two-thousand, something like that, but yeah, just book money.

Rockell: So how would you say that student loans have impacted your life?

Michael: Right after high school, it was definitely impactful because the rate of what I had to pay when I was in school quadrupled, and then me, again at a young age, ignoring my obligations, thinking, eh, I'll deal with it later or I'm not working, and ignoring it, and then penalties and things tripling up, and before you know it, you're looking at almost a mortgage. So, yeah, I was kind of just trying to think about not looking at it, thinking it's going to go away, but it's not, right?

Rockell: Right.

Michael: So financially, it took money from me every month because I was trying to do the right thing by paying on it. But as I paid on it, I would see no dent at all in the loan; the more I would pay, the more it would grow. It just didn't make sense to me. So, you just get very disheartened about the whole situation and just frustrated that there's no way out.

Rockell: No way out until you pay it off.

Michael: Yeah, exactly.

Rockell: Have you paid off your loans, or are you still paying on them?

Michael: Oh, I paid it off. I made it my mission. I did a couple good deals at work, and I was able to just pay it off in a lump sum. It hurt writing a check, but it also felt great.

Rockell: How did you feel when you were able to write that check and pay it off?

Michael: Oh, felt blessed, definitely felt blessed. It was a dream of just getting that burden off of me—it was bittersweet. I'm not even going to say I did backflips because it hurt. I hate to say giving away all this money, but I feel, to some extent, I did throw away a lot of that money. So, it was bittersweet as far as I'm throwing away money, but then the positive was just one more person off my back.

Rockell: Right, I totally understand. So, what is your advice to students trying to figure out how to afford college? What would you tell those students right now?

Michael: Well, again, since the world is what it is, very technology-based and there are so many forms of alternative education, I would really encourage students to really just do research on what they have an interest in. Because more than likely, there is some resource that they can probably use for free to know if that's something they actually have an interest in before wasting a lot of time and money with our traditional college classes. So yeah, I would just say have them explore free resources and maybe talk with a mentor before they go down that shoot because college isn't for everyone. So, it just really depends on the individual.

#4 Odell Bizzell II

Rockell: Odell, what did you major in?

Odell: I majored in communication.

Rockell: Prior to going to college, what was your game plan to pay for college?

Odell: My game plan was always to get scholarships. My dad went to a military school where they paid him, basically, to go to school. My mother immigrated from West Africa, and she got grants and scholarships to go to school because she was a TRIO student. So, I never thought, "Oh, I'm going to have to pay for school." I always thought I would get good enough grades, get scholarships, and I would go to college that way. That's how I would pay for it.

Rockell: Okay, and did it work out the way that you expected?

Odell: The first year. So, I graduated from high school, eighth in my class, and got more than enough scholarship money. I just got to school and got super lazy and lost focus. It was my first time away from home. So, I stayed out as late as I wanted to. I was always (air quotes) really smart, always a really good student. I just thought it would translate to college, but it didn't. I was always the charismatic high school student. If I didn't get something in on time, Ms. Anderson would say, "Oh, okay. All right, Odell. You're great, you're great. You're fine. You'll do it." But in college it was like, "Nope, Nope." And so, I lost my scholarship in my freshman year, and I was going to quit school because, like I said before, I only knew about scholarships. Then I discovered the devil. The devil by the name of student loans.

Rockell: Do you remember approximately how much you took out in student loans?

Odell: Yes. So, I've always been entrepreneurially-minded. And so, for the student reading this, I just want to tell you that the way you think things will work money-wise, they might work, but it might take longer than you think. I always knew I was going to make a lot of money. I just didn't know how and I didn't know when. And so, when I got the student loans, there was an option to get federal funding and, or, private funding. I think I came up in college during the wild, wild west of student loans. Where it was, "Hey, how much money do you want, kid? We'll give it to you." And it was like, "You can get this much, and it'll cover exactly what you need, or you can get this much."

I always chose the maximum amount. I got the maximum amount of private student loans because I was like, "Well, shoot. I can get an extra $5,000, flip it, and do all these things I was thinking about doing." So, I got the maximum amount of student loans every year, and I ended up borrowing like $60,000 total when I only needed $30,000.

Rockell: Wow, so how would you do things differently? Knowing what you know today?

Odell: Well, there are two things; I would've treated school like a job, and not an adventure. I would've just gone to school, focused on getting maximum scholarship money. You can get scholarships even when you're in school. That's something I didn't know at the time, because I wasn't really focused on school. Every student should know that college is a job where you can have fun. It's a job where you can schedule your fun time, hang out with friends, and live life. But it's a job. You have a duty to do when you go to school; and your duty is to get the best grades possible and to become the most qualified graduate that you can be. That's your job. That's what you have to do. That's your focus. I would've done that. The second thing I would've done is, I would've never gotten more student loans than I needed. If I would've done the first thing, I wouldn't have had to get student loans anyway. But I absolutely would have never gotten more than what I needed. Because when you get into student loan debt, you're basically hedging that your degree will make you more money than that loan payment. And you have no idea if that's true or not. You don't know what the economy's going to do. You don't know. So, I would get the minimum amount of student loans that I needed. That's the second thing I would've done.

Rockell: How has taking out student loans impacted your life?

Odell: Mental health-wise, it's like having a bounty on your head. Because, I borrowed $60,000, but let's just be honest, there's a whole lot more that was owed on that. When you know you have that hanging over your head, you can never be comfortable mentally. You go to the bank and you try to ask for a car loan, and you're thinking, "Wow. Are they going to not give it to me because I have all of this student loan debt?"

It's a mental weight. And fortunately for me, I've always had high aspirations. And so, I could look at however much it was and say, "Okay. I can eventually get to that." But even with that, being young, if you want to start a family, it'll hinder that. If you want to buy a home and settle somewhere, it'll hinder that. If you want to get an apartment, it hinders all of that. And that's not what you think about, because they made it so easy to get student loans. So, it definitely hinders your mental health and your financial growth because, instead of putting money away to invest for the long term, you're paying student loans.

Rockell: What is your advice to students trying to figure out how to afford college?

Odell: Be resourceful. Don't think about it like, "Well, I can only go this way or that way." Be resourceful. Plan out the options. Look at it from the perspective of, "I can get scholarships." It's better to work hard on the front end, getting scholarships, than to work hard on the back end, trying to find a job to pay off bad student loans. The pain of regret is way heavier than the pain of discipline. So, be disciplined on the front end and find scholarships because they're out there. I dare to say that if you don't find the scholarships, it's because you didn't put in the time and effort to get them. The second thing is, make student loans your last resort. Your very last resort. If you have a dream school that you want to go to, put off the dream school and go to community college. Do whatever you can to not have to pay back student loans. I say this in jest: student loans are the devil. That means I'm being funny, but in every "Just kidding," there's a little seriousness to it.

#5 Ron Hariprashad

Rockell: Ron, can you tell me what it is that you majored in?

Ron: My bachelor's is in environmental engineering, and I didn't finish my master's. But I went and did two years of my master's for geosciences in hydro-geology.

Rockell: Are you currently working in the field in which you got your degree?

Ron: Yeah. I'm a water resources engineer, but specifically for roadway design.

Rockell: Nice and prior to going to college, what was your game plan to pay for your education?

Ron: I wanted to be fully covered through scholarships. I applied for FAFSA to get a lot of Pell grants and Bright Futures scholarships. I also got a few science scholarships that helped me pay to go to any school in the state. That was a state-run system. So that included UCF and FIU for tuition, though, just tuition.

Rockell: Okay, and with all the money that you got through the scholarships, grants, and FAFSA, was that enough to cover everything that you needed to be covered?

Ron: It covered tuition and housing when I was at UCF, but it didn't cover food.

Rockell: So why did you take out the loan?

Ron: It was for my … and maybe I could have done it better when I was younger, but the meal plan. I needed to eat, but I wasn't the best cook growing up, so I never thought about that stuff. So, I did it for the meal plan.

Rockell: Knowing what you know now, how would you have done things differently?

Ron: I grew up in Miami. I've been here my whole life. But I would have gone to Miami Dade College for a year, or two years, or whatever it took. Probably saved more money, learned how to cook, and then moved out. But yeah, I would've flipped the script and stayed for two years then moved instead of leaving and then moving back home.

Rockell: Okay, and once you took out the loan, did you realize you were going to need more loans? And then what did you do after that?

Ron: Yeah, so I realized I'd have to do that every year just to have a consistent way of eating if I wanted to stay healthy and fit. That's when I was like, "I can go home and my parents can take care of this." Also, with the housing money I had, I was like, "Okay, it can go into my bank account versus me paying UCF. I'd rather just have it for my own use."

Rockell: How much in total did you take out for your loan?

Ron: It was $3,300. That covered the meal plan for fall and spring.

Rockell: Would you say that this loan has impacted your life in any way, shape, or form?

Ron: Yeah, I think it was, honestly, a positive thing. It taught me a lot about finances, and that's what I tell kids. I'm like, "College is a good way to learn to just talk about finances." Because I talked to my dad, I'm like, "Hey, it doesn't really make sense." And my dad's always been good with finances. It was that weird moment in life where I kind of became an adult. I'm like, "This makes no sense. I'm paying all this money and you guys are home, and you guys offered me to come back home." So, it was a positive thing, I think.

Rockell: I like that your experience, even though it was negative, as far as taking out the money, it taught you that this probably isn't the best route and that there was actually a better route at home waiting for you.

Ron: Yeah, and I know everyone doesn't have that option.

Rockell: Right, but at least you utilized what you had, which is great. How long did it take you to pay off your loan? Or are you still paying it off?

Ron: It took me a total of six years to pay it off. While I was in college, I was only paying $10 a week, $40 a month just to keep the interest from piling up. Then, when I got my first real full-time job as a professional engineer, I paid it off with part of my signing bonus.

Rockell: What is your advice to students trying to figure out how to afford college?

Ron: Apply for scholarships and other government funding. Then the second thing I would say is don't take shame in taking longer to finish college. I think working while you're in college and possibly paying for your own classes or whatever it is, that does a lot for you as a young adult. Working helps you a lot. Don't be ashamed of taking longer while you're working.

17.

What Is Your Game Plan?

Now that you've read through this entire book, I want to challenge you to create your own game plan to pay for college. Use the blank space below and the next couple of pages to write down the strategies you're going to implement and what it's going to take in order for these strategies to work. Do you need to improve your grades, participate in tutoring, study before your test, participate in extracurricular activities, actually believe in yourself, create a GoFundMe page, research, make time for scholarships? What do you need to do? If you're still not sure, take this book to your counselor, advisor, or parent and ask for help in creating your game plan. When you're done, take a picture of the pages you wrote on and send it to me at thescholarbudget@gmail.com or dm/tag me @thescholarbudget.

You got this, friend!

Game Plan Notes

Game Plan Notes

Game Plan Notes

About The Author

Rockell Bartoli has spoken to thousands of students and has delivered empowering messages for notable organizations such as TRIO, Burger King's McLamore Foundation, and Carnival Cruise Line's Scholarship and Mentoring Program.

Prior to becoming a professional speaker and author, her role as a school counselor allowed her to help teens and young adults identify their career path and the right tools to reach their most important life goals. Rockell grew up the product of a single mother and was raised by her grandmother. Using the goal-setting strategies she shares in her presentations, she became one of the first people in her family to obtain a bachelor's degree in education and a master's degree in school guidance and counseling.

In her spare time, Rockell loves traveling with her family, therapeutic trips to Target, and watching a good Netflix series with her hubby.

Made in the USA
Columbia, SC
22 May 2022

60691044R00083